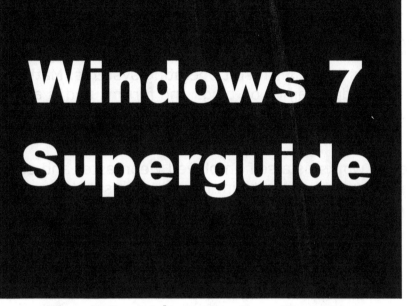

By Matthew A. Buxton

About the Author

Matthew A. Buxton holds a degree in computer studies and has several years experience working in programming and technical support. He is the author and webmaster of the popular Windows website Top-Windows-Tutorials.com and has written several articles about Microsoft operating systems. Matthew also writes about video games on blogs and forums and is a passionate game player across several different formats.

He currently works as a self employed webmaster and computer consultant. You can contact him by visiting his website, http://www.Top-Windows-Tutorials.com/

Authors Acknowledgements

First and foremost, I'd like to thank my family, especially my mother whose tireless dedication to proof reading and checking has made this book into the professional document that it is.

Secondly, I'd like to thank the folks at SBI, (http://www.sitesell.com/Matthew77.html) for their superb small business internet hosting service. Without you guys, I would probably still be bogged down in the technical details of single-handedly running a professional website and this book would never have been produced. Instead, I am adding content on a weekly basis and flying high in the search engine rankings!

I would also like to thank Seniornet New Zealand for helping to fund the writing of this book and for their input and suggestions.

Finally, I want to thank you, for purchasing my book and (hopefully!) visiting my website. I sincerely hope you will find the material easy to understand and that it helps you get the best out of your Windows 7 computer.

Table of Contents

Foreword

The foreword of a book about a new version of Windows is a great chance for venerable technical authors to get nostalgic. When technical authors of the future look back on the launch of Windows 7, they will almost certainly note it as a turning point in the fortunes of Microsoft's operating system. Even though Windows 7 has only been out a few months as I type this, the sales figures strongly suggest that Microsoft is on to a winner.

My own experience with Windows began with Windows 3.11, back in 1994. I remember being distinctly unimpressed with the operating systems sluggish performance and extravagant (for the time) system requirements. There was no way I would swap my zippy Commodore Amiga computer for one of those infernal PC contraptions, or so I thought.

Even back in the days of Windows 3, Microsoft was making headway into the home computer market and already beginning to dominate the business computer market. Windows PC's had high resolution graphics as standard and while this did mean that you could not use your television as a cheap alternative to a dedicated monitor, it meant that productivity software on the PC had an advantage from the start. Thanks to some aggressive marketing, it was not long before Windows was the standard home computer operating system and all its competitors (bar one, Apple Mac OS) fell by the wayside.

In 2001, Microsoft introduced Windows XP. Windows XP brought about huge improvements in stability and performance over its predecessors, Windows ME and Windows 98. After a few grumbles from disgruntled early adopters who found some software to be incompatible, XP was taken up and loved by the Windows computing masses. With superb support for multimedia and games and good performance on a wide range of hardware, XP was a resounding success.

While far from being perfect (especially where security is concerned) Windows XP's popularity is still indisputable. With the launch of Windows Vista, Microsoft introduced new security features to the operating system (such as UAC, User Account Control) and radically altered the way other OS components worked. XP users the world over were shocked, suddenly, this new upstart operating system seemed to offer no tangible benefits over Windows XP and a whole heap of compatibility problems, not to mention new annoyances from the improved security features. Despite improvements issued by Microsoft after Vista launched, the troubled operating system could not shake off its bad reputation.

With Windows 7, Microsoft knew that they had to pull out all the stops. If the users did not see real, obvious benefits to upgrading to the new operating system, it would be written off as another Vista. Furthermore, Vista had gained the reputation of being slow, unwieldy and crippled with poor compatibility. While features like User Account Control and the loss of some backward compatibility are necessary to keep the operating system evolving, it was obvious that Windows 7 needed to offer something more. Some drastic performance improvements and some fantastic new features were needed to finally convince the die-hard XP fans to take the plunge. Microsoft really needed to make Windows 7 something special...

...I think they just might have succeeded!

Introduction

Welcome to our newest Top-Windows-Tutorials.com Superguide. After the success of our OpenOffice.org Writer Superguide, there was a lot of interest in the possibility of a Windows 7 Superguide. With Windows 7 mere months old, it was the perfect time to produce a guide for new users. Creating a Superguide for a whole operating system has been a much bigger task than the OpenOffice.org writer Superguide. At over twice the size of the first Superguide, we hope you will be pleased with the results.

About this book (physical book edition)

The Windows 7 Superguide was originally designed as a complete training course, this included video content as well as an e-book. This physical book edition was designed for those of you who wanted the convenience of being able to access the material in a more traditional format. The full version of Windows 7 Superguide, which runs on your desktop PC and includes full video tutorials too, makes an excellent accompaniment to this book. To find out more, visit this page on our website:- http://www.top-windows-tutorials.com/windows-7-superguide.html

Prerequisites

Apart from a desire to learn about Windows 7, there are a few things you should have before you start this course.

You should know some basic computer skills, such as how to turn your machine on. Knowing how to operate a keyboard and mouse is also very useful.

If you are not familiar with using computers of any kind, you may want to see Microsoft's guide to using menus, buttons, bars and boxes. You can access this guide in two ways. If you have an internet connection, you can visit this page:-
http://windows.microsoft.com/en-US/windows-vista/Using-menus-buttons-bars-and-boxes.

If you are not connected to the internet, you can also find the guide (and lots of other helpful hints and tips) in the Windows 7 help files. Open the Start Menu by clicking on it once and then click on "Help and Support". See the picture below for an example:-

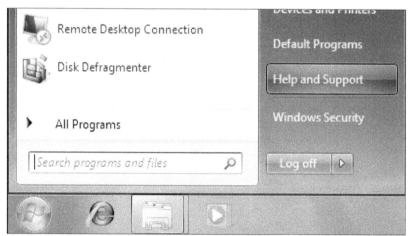

Accessing help and support on a Windows 7 machine

The Help and Support window will then open. At the top of the window is a search box. Click on this box once with the mouse pointer and then enter "using menus buttons bars and boxes". Click on the magnifying glass icon, you should then see the following window:-

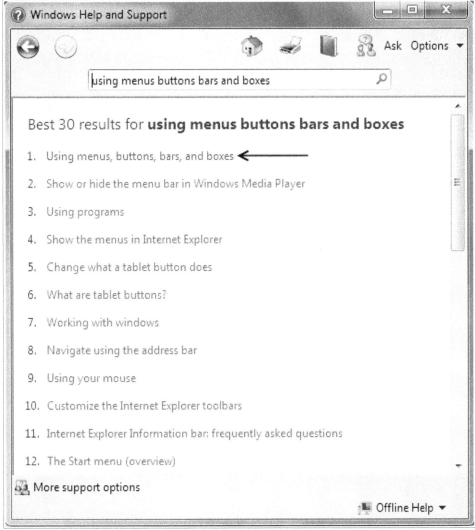

There are lots of helpful articles in Windows Help and Support

To read the article, simply click on it from the list.

Access to a Windows 7 machine, while not absolutely essential, is also extremely helpful for practising your skills.

Conventions used in this book

We have aimed to keep this book free of jargon and technical terms wherever possible. One convention we did decide on is regarding the use of the mouse. This book is written assuming a right handed mouse configuration. When we instruct you to click on an item, we are talking about clicking with the primary mouse button. When we talk about right-clicking, we mean the secondary mouse button. We did consider using different terminology, such as "alt click" or something similar, but nothing was as clear as simply using "click" and "right click". We hope left handed users will forgive us this bias.

Chapter 1 – The Beginning

It is time to start your journey. A whole new, exciting modern operating system holds so many possibilities for you and your PC. A home computer is such a versatile tool, from painting pictures to writing books to making websites and playing games, there are hundreds of exciting tasks Windows 7 can help you with. So, without further ado, let the Windows 7 Superguide begin!

Before You Begin

The launch of a new Microsoft operating system is always a busy time for Microsoft's marketing department and the release of Windows 7 is no exception. Eager to repair some of the damage done when Windows Vista launched, Windows 7 is here to save Microsoft's reputation. Windows 7 should finally replace the venerable but much loved Windows XP as the favourite desktop OS of millions of users worldwide. Let's take a sober look at Windows 7 and what it brings to the table for home users.

What is Windows 7?

Windows 7 builds on the good features of Windows Vista as well as introducing many new features of its own. It is not a completely rewritten version of Windows (this would probably be impossible within a three year timespan), rather a refined, enhanced and polished update. Many early adopters say it is everything Windows Vista should have been and more.

Windows 7 has been designed to be faster, easier and more fun to use than Windows Vista was. If you have used Windows before, you will learn how completing basic tasks like switching between applications is now faster and easier than ever before. If you have never used Windows before, you will be delighted to know that you are joining us for what many users consider to be the best version of Windows yet.

Do I need Windows 7?

If you are reading this guide then we will assume that you have already purchased Windows 7 or you are strongly considering an upgrade. If you are planning to purchase a new Windows PC, you should absolutely make sure that it ships with Windows 7 already installed. If you are planning to upgrade your existing computer, things are a little more complicated but we will discuss the options later on in this chapter.

Choosing the right version

Buying Windows 7, either pre-installed or as an upgrade to an existing PC, might not be as straightforward as you think. There are a total of six different versions of Windows 7 available and each (apart from one) is available in 32 bit and 64 bit versions, but more on those later. For home users, the correct choice is usually Home Premium edition, but we'll take a look now at each version of the operating system and describe what it offers.

Windows 7 Starter:- This version of Windows 7 is a light-weight, basic version designed for lower end portable computers. It lacks many of the advanced features such as the ability to play DVD's or to use Windows fancy Aero Glass desktop (Aero glass uses the power of modern graphics cards to make your desktop look really stunning, it also helps with several new Windows 7 features that you will discover as you follow this guide). This version is only available pre-installed with certain PC's. It is suitable for home users who want to carry out basic computing tasks such as light internet use or basic word processing.

Windows 7 Home Basic:- This version is similar to the Starter edition but includes a few more features. It has been designed for emerging markets, that is countries which are rapidly expanding their economies. Windows 7 Home Basic edition is not available in Australia, Canada, France, Germany, Ireland, The Netherlands, United Arab Emirates, Saudi Arabia, New Zealand, the United States or the United Kingdom. Where available, Home Basic edition is a reasonable way to get Windows 7 for older computers if you are on a tight budget, but most users will be better off with the Home Premium edition.

Windows 7 Home Premium:- This is the version that most home users will choose. It includes the full Windows Aero interface experience, as well as Windows Media Player and

Windows Media Center. Most computers sold to home users will come pre-installed with this version.

Windows 7 Professional:- This is the version targeted at enthusiasts and IT professionals. It includes all the features of the Home Premium edition as well as the ability to join a Windows Server Domain. This could be an important feature if you need to use your computer at work, you should ask your IT department for more information. Professional edition also includes the encrypting file system and Windows XP mode, which we mention briefly in lesson 28.3.

Windows 7 Enterprise:- This edition includes all the available features plus additional features designed for business customers use, such as Bitlocker drive encryption and UNIX application support. It is only available to business customers who have special volume license agreements with Microsoft.

Windows 7 Ultimate:- The Ultimate edition is for the man or woman who simply has to have it all. Yes, this version includes everything, all available features. It's actually the same as the Enterprise edition only this version will be available to all customers and not just businesses. If you are planning on buying this version you might be interested to know that there are no "ultimate extras" this time around. In Windows Vista, the Ultimate edition received several bonus features and downloads that the other versions never got, this isn't going to happen with Windows 7.

If you're still confused as to which version you need, then chances are that Home Premium is the right version for you. If the extra features that come with the Professional and Ultimate editions sounded like another language to you then it is unlikely you will ever need them. If you do, it is possible to upgrade through Windows Anytime Upgrade, as long as you have an internet connection and a means of electronic payment such as a credit card. Be warned though, the prices for Anytime Upgrade are not always as economical as simply buying the correct version of Windows in the first place.

32 bit or 64 bit?

When discussing this subject, it is easy for technical authors such as myself to begin reminiscing about our childhoods and the amount of memory and storage space the early computers of the time had. I decided I would spare you that this time and get to the point. 64 bit versions of Windows can access more memory than their 32 bit counterparts, but the 32 bit versions tend to have better overall compatibility especially with older hardware and software. The 32 bit versions of Windows 7 can access a maximum of 4 gigabytes of RAM. RAM is the primary storage area on your computer that Windows uses for programs and data that it is currently working on. It is not the same as the hard drive which is used to store programs and data that are not currently being used. If you're confused, we will discuss these terms in more detail later, when we talk about choosing a computer for Windows 7 or upgrading an existing machine.

The 64 bit versions of Windows 7 can access either 16gb on Home Premium or up to a whopping 192 gigabytes on Professional, Enterprise and Ultimate editions. Again, I want to tell you how many hundreds of times more capacity that is than the first hard drive I owned, but I wont.

Now, 4 Gigabytes of memory might seem like a lot and for many users it will be more than adequate. However, it is important to note that this maximum memory allocation includes memory on your graphics card too. Were you to purchase a high end graphics card for gaming, with 1 gigabyte of memory, the most memory you could then use with a 32 bit version of Windows would be 3 gigabytes. With graphics cards now shipping with even more memory than that and with top-spec gaming motherboards giving the option of attaching two or more graphics cards at once, enthusiasts might need to seriously consider going 64 bit to get the most out of their machines. Regular home users can safely stay 32 bit for the foreseeable future, however.

Unlike previous versions of Windows, Windows 7 Home

Premium, Professional and Ultimate editions will ship with both 32 bit and 64 bit versions in the same box. However, you can't switch between versions without either reinstalling your operating system or configuring some kind of dual booting system, but more on that later.

Taking the plunge

So, you have decided on which edition of Windows 7 to purchase, how do you go about getting it? Before you tear off to the store with your shopping list, let's look at a couple of options.

The easy way - Choosing a new computer with Windows 7 installed

Buying a computer with Windows 7 pre-installed is the easiest way to get the operating system. The hard part is done and you can get right on with discovering your new PC. Which PC you choose is largely down to your personal tastes and requirements. Do your homework, look for reviews on the internet if possible and think carefully before parting with your cash. Here are a few pointers to look out for when buying a Windows 7 PC.

Memory:– Windows 7 requires 1 gigabyte of memory, also called RAM. RAM is where the computer stores programs and data it is currently working on, this is different to the hard disk which is generally only fast enough to store programs and data you are not currently using. One gigabyte of memory is adequate for regular computing tasks such as surfing the internet, word-processing or writing e-mails. If you work with lots of programs at once, or you do more demanding tasks on your computer such as gaming, you may want to go for a machine with 2 or more gigabytes of memory. Memory can easily be upgraded in almost all computers, including laptops.

Hard Drive Capacity:– Your hard drive is used to store all the programs and data you keep on your PC. Hard drive sizes are measured in gigabytes too, but they are considerably larger than memory or RAM capacities. Windows 7 requires 16 gigabytes of hard drive space all to itself. The remaining space is filled up with any other programs you install and any files you create yourself or download from the internet. If you have a large collection of multimedia files, you will want to make sure to purchase a machine with an equally large hard drive. Don't forget that hard drives are mechanical devices and prone to sudden, random failures. Always keep a backup of your data if it is important, we discuss backup and the Windows 7 backup utility in chapter 5.

Graphics Card:– The graphics card or graphics chip in the computer you buy is often overlooked by consumers when shopping for a new computer. You should make sure to check that the graphics card in the machine is capable of running Windows Aero desktop, you will see why in later lessons. If you plan to play the latest games on your machine, you will need a PC with a more powerful graphics chip. Be sure to budget for this and check the requirements for the games you want to play to make sure your new PC matches up.

All shapes and sizes:– Modern PC's come in all kinds of different shapes and sizes, from tiny ultra-portables to huge, powerful desktops. Again, the machine you choose comes down to personal taste and requirements. As a general rule, desktop computers have better upgrade options, larger displays and give more "bang for the buck" in terms of performance. Laptop, netbook (very small laptops, sometimes called ultra portables) and tablet PC's can, obviously, be transported and used almost anywhere. That could be up and down the country as you travel on business or up and down the house and garden as you work and play at home. Laptops and ultra-portables also take up less space but aren't quite so suited to heavy computing work as desktop PC's are and the smaller the PC gets the less powerful it is likely to be.

The hard way – Upgrading an existing computer

Windows 7 is a compelling upgrade for many existing computers too, particularly for those die-hard Windows XP users who want to take advantage of the newer features that Windows 7 brings. Upgrading an existing computer to Windows 7 is a little more tricky than just going out and buying one with Windows 7 preloaded. Care must be taken to backup all your data and you may have to reinstall all of your programs once you have finished upgrading your operating system.

Custom install versus in-place upgrade

There are two ways in which you can change operating systems on your PC, custom install and in-place upgrade. An in-place upgrade changes your current operating system from one version to another. So, in theory at least, all you need to do is insert the Windows 7 DVD and wait for the process to complete. In practise it is not always that simple. Problems can and do occur since no two Windows installations are exactly alike. Many IT professionals prefer to do a custom installation instead. You should definitely make sure that you have a full backup of your system before you begin.

When you perform a custom installation, your entire existing operating system is removed and replaced with the new one. Usually during this process, you will lose any programs and data that you have not backed up. This is the big disadvantage of a custom installation.

When choosing which type of installation to perform, in lots of cases, Microsoft have already made the decision for you. If you are upgrading from Windows XP, you only have the choice of a custom installation. Similarly if you are upgrading from a 32 bit version of Windows to a 64 bit version then a custom installation is also the only way to go. If you have Windows Vista Home Basic or Home Premium, then you can in-place upgrade to Windows 7 Home Premium, Professional or Ultimate. However, if you have Windows Vista Ultimate, you can only in-place upgrade to Windows 7 Ultimate.

Is my old PC capable of running Windows 7?

Windows 7 requires a 1 gigahertz processor and 1 gigabyte of RAM (2 gigabytes for the 64 bit version). You will also need a DirectX 9 graphics device. The easiest way to see if your computer meets these requirements is to obtain the Windows 7 upgrade advisor. This free piece of software scans software and hardware in your system and lets you know about any potential problems before you reach into your wallet. You can download it for free here **http://tinyurl.com/mnmj8u.**

Is that all?

We did consider covering installation and upgrading to Windows 7 in this guide. However, we decided that it was beyond the scope of a book aimed at beginners. We would want to cover dual booting (installing two or more operating systems at once) and various other options to really cover the subject in the kind of detail that Superguide readers would expect. If you want to upgrade your existing computer to Windows 7, discuss the options with a local IT professional or computer workshop. They will be able to asses all your upgrade options.

Lesson 1 – Diving In

1.1 Introduction to the Desktop

In our first video, we give you a quick tour of the Windows 7 desktop. This should have been at least somewhat familiar to those of you who have used Windows before. Let us take a look at the elements of the desktop, figure 1.1 shows them:-

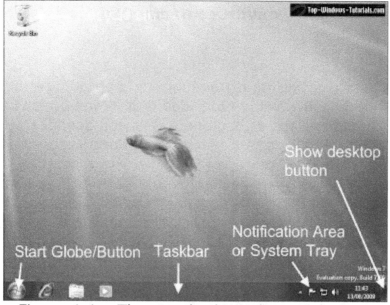

Figure 1.1 – The standard Windows 7 desktop

Figure 1.1 shows the standard Windows 7 desktop you will see on a clean (new) installation of the operating system. We'll go over the basic elements shown in the picture.

Start Globe/button:- Windows Vista users will be familiar with a Start Globe, whereas XP users will be more familiar with the Start Button. This is the main starting point for most activities on your computer because it opens the Start Menu. Clicking it once opens up the Start Menu and clicking it again closes it. From the Start Menu you can access all the programs installed on your computer.

Taskbar:- The area at the bottom between the Start Globe and the Notification Area is called the Taskbar. The Taskbar works a little differently to both Windows XP and Windows Vista. To the right of the Start Globe you may have noticed some icons. If you are familiar with earlier versions of Windows you will know that the Taskbar is where you can see programs that are already running. You might be worried as to why there appears to be programs already running. Well, these programs are not actually running at all. Unlike earlier versions of Windows, programs can be "pinned" on the Taskbar. This means that they will stay on the Taskbar for easy access even when they are not running. By default, from left to right we get Internet Explorer, Windows Explorer and Windows Media Player. This might be different on your version of Windows 7 depending on whereabouts you live in the world and which version of Windows 7 you have installed.

It is important to understand that icons on the Taskbar do not necessarily represent programs that are running. You can click on the icons pinned to the Taskbar to start the program running. When a program is running, it will have a border around its Taskbar icon, see figure 1.2 for an example:-

Figure 1.2 – Internet Explorer running on the Taskbar, next to Windows Explorer which is "pinned" but not running

If you hover your mouse pointer over a running Taskbar icon, Windows will show you a preview window:-

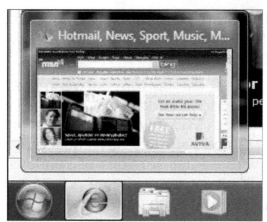

Figure 1.3 – Hover your mouse pointer over a program running on the Taskbar to see a preview of the window

You can click on the preview window to go directly to the application. (This feature is only available if your PC is running the Aero Glass interface).

Notification Area or System Tray:- The official Microsoft name for this part of the desktop is the Notification Area, but lots of users refer to it as the System Tray. Whatever you choose to call it, it has changed significantly in Windows 7. To see your System Tray icons, you now click the small up pointing arrow. See figure 1.4 for more details.

Figure 1.4 – The new Notification Area/System Tray is opened with a click on this small arrow icon

If you are not sure what the Notification Area is for, do not worry, we cover it in more detail in lesson 14.

To the right of the arrow icon highlighted in Figure 1.4, there are three other icons. These icons are also counted as part of the Notification Area, though you might think otherwise at first glance. The flag shaped icon is the Action Center. This notifies you about potential problems on your PC, such as security alerts. Next to that is the network icon, this can be used for connecting quickly to networks, both wired and wireless. Then there's the volume icon, a quick click of this accesses a sliding control which can adjust the volume level for all sounds on your computer.

Date and time:- To the right of the Notification Area (see figure 1.1) is the date and time display. This is fairly self explanatory. You can click on the date and time display down here to adjust your computers clock if it is not showing the correct time.

Show Desktop button:- Clicking in the very bottom right hand corner of the Windows 7 desktop will activate the Show Desktop button. This button hides all of your open windows so that you can see the desktop. Clicking it again will reveal the windows again.

Recycle Bin:- This lonely looking icon in the top left hand corner of the desktop is the Recyle Bin. Files and folders you delete are (usually!) placed in this folder before being removed entirely. We cover this in more detail in lesson 10.

Note:- The picture of the fish in the background on our desktop is called the Desktop Background or Wallpaper. This picture can be changed to any image you like and we show you how in lesson 29. Many of our videos and lessons were compiled using a pre release version of Windows 7 and the standard Desktop Background was changed for the release version. Because of this, don't be alarmed if your desktop background looks different.

If you have never used Windows before, you might be confused as to what all these different components do. Lesson 1 was really to give you an overview of the components and not what they do, so move along to lesson 2 where we look at the Start Menu, probably the most important component to master on your Windows 7 machine.

Lesson 2 – Exploring The Start Menu

2.1 - Introducing the Start Menu

The Start Menu is usually the first place you go to when you want to do something on your computer. From the Start Menu you can launch programs, search for files, change settings and get help. In lesson 1 we showed you how to open the Start Menu by clicking on the Start Globe. Figure 2.1 shows an open Start Menu:-

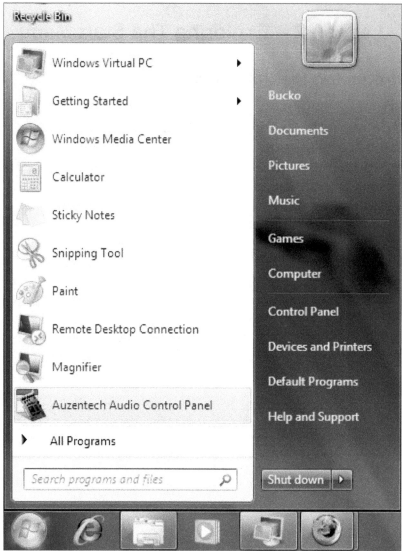

Figure 2.1 – The Start Menu on a Windows 7 machine, the icons you see on your machine may be different in some places

The Windows 7 Start Menu will be familiar to Windows Vista users but may look a little different to Windows XP users. At the top of the Start Menu there are some recently used items. Items with an arrow to the right of them have a sub-menu. In figure 2.1 we can see that Getting Started and Windows Virtual

PC both have arrows indicating sub-menus. To open a sub-menu, simply hover over the icon with your mouse pointer. Figure 2.2 shows the sub-menu items for "Getting Started".

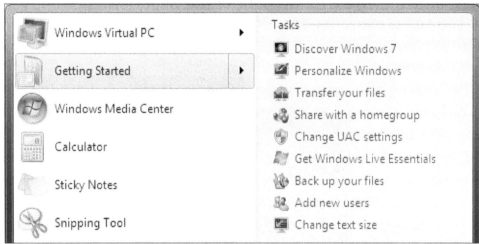

Figure 2.2 – Opening the sub-menu for the "Getting Started" item

Now, you can click the individual items to jump directly to those specific tasks, such as "Discover Windows 7" or "Personalize Windows". Alternatively, you can click the "Getting started" icon on the left to open the Getting Started Control Panel item. Sub-menus on the Start Menu are referred to as "Jump Lists".

Referring back to figure 2.1 for a moment, on the right of the Start Menu, we have some short cuts to key places or items in the operating system. The first four items from the top let us jump directly to our own personal folders. We will explore these folders in more detail in lesson 4. We can also explore the Computer (this was "My Computer" on Windows XP) and change various settings in the Control Panel or various other places, or get Help and Support.

2.2 - Shut down options

At the very bottom of the Start Menu is the Shut down button. Clicking that will shut down and power off your computer. If you hover over the arrow to the right of the Shut down button, you will see some extra options, figure 2.3 shows the available options:-

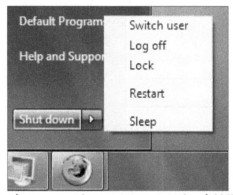

Figure 2.3 – Shut down options on a typical Windows 7 machine

The shut down options are as follows:-

Switch user:- This allows you to change user accounts. Windows 7 machines can have multiple user accounts where each user has their own unique settings and personal documents folders. We cover this in detail in lesson 21.

Log off:- This will shut down your user account but not turn off the machine. You would do this if you wanted to let another person use the PC. Again, this is covered in more detail in lesson 21.

Lock:- If you need to leave your computer for a moment and want to make sure that nobody else takes over and starts tinkering with the programs and data you are working with, choose this option. You can then unlock your computer when you return by entering your password. We show you how to set passwords in lesson 21.4.

Restart:- Makes your computer reboot or restart. Closes down all open files and programs first. You should use this option rather than pressing the reset button on your PC or turning it off at the wall.

Sleep:- Puts your computer into a low-power standby mode. When you wake your computer from sleep mode it will restart more quickly than if you had powered it down completely. A word of warning, some hardware is not fully compatible with sleep mode and may not work correctly when the computer is awoken again. To restore functionality you will need to use the restart option.

2.3 - Using search to run software or open files

You will recall we said that the Start Menu is a launchpad for other software on your PC. How do we launch software if it's not on the list of items we can see in figure 2.1? The most common way to launch programs is by typing the name of the program into the search box. To start Spider Solitaire, for instance, simply entered "spider" into the search box, figure 2.4 illustrates this:-

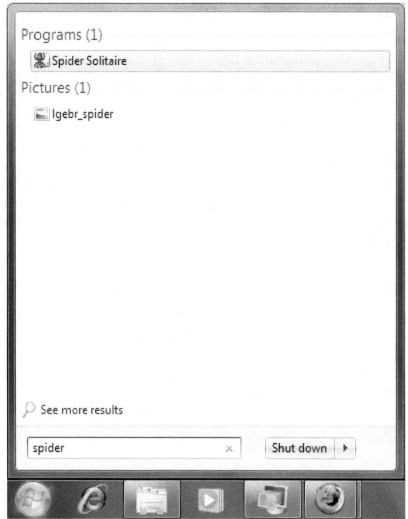

*Figure 2.4 – Searching for an item on the Start Menu. Note how
the search result finds software (programs) and a picture file*

Notice how searching for "spider" in figure 2.4 also found a
picture file. Searching like this actually finds pictures,
documents and other files too. To open a program, picture or
any other type of file, click it once.

2.4 - Browsing the Start Menu and other options

It is also possible to browse the Start Menu in the 'old fashioned way', that is by clicking on (or hovering over) "All Programs" and browsing to the program you want to run yourself. If you are used to Windows XP you will notice that when you do this, the Start Menu items do not fly out over the screen any more. Instead, you simply get a list of your programs, as was the case in Windows Vista. If you click on a sub-folder it expands out. To run a program, click on it once.

If you right click on an icon, a new menu will appear (known as a context menu). In this menu we have some extra options to explore. Figure 2.5 shows the context menu:-

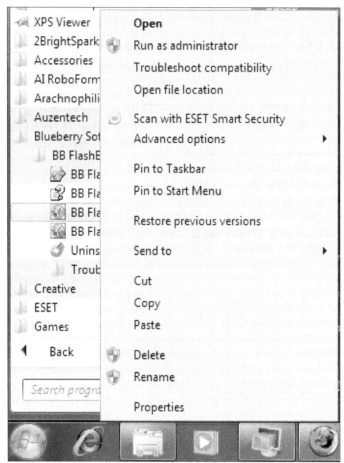

Figure 2.5 – The context menu appears when you right click on an icon

This menu has lots of intimidating looking options, but the only two we want to discuss in this lesson are "Pin to Taskbar" and "Pin to Start Menu".

If you choose "Pin to Start Menu", the icon will be attached to the top of the Start Menu. Refer back to figure 2.1, the icon would appear right at the top of the Start Menu above "Windows Virtual PC". The icon would be permanently pinned to the top of the Start Menu, unlike the most recently used icons which will appear below it. These items will gradually be replaced by other programs that you use more often. You can use the Pin to Start Menu facility for favourite or important programs. To unpin an icon, simply right click on it and choose "Unpin from Start Menu".

The Pin to Taskbar option will permanently pin the icon to the Taskbar, even when it is not running. Recall in lesson 1 we saw Internet Explorer, Windows Explorer and Windows Media Player on the Taskbar, even though they were not running. You can 'pin' any icon you choose to the Taskbar by using this option.

You can also "pin" items to the Desktop (the area where the Recycle Bin sits all on its own initially) though in line with earlier versions of Windows this is called creating a shortcut. To do this, right click on an icon on the Start Menu (either one you searched for or browsed to) and choose "Send To" then choose "Desktop (create shortcut)". Figure 2.6 illustrates this:-

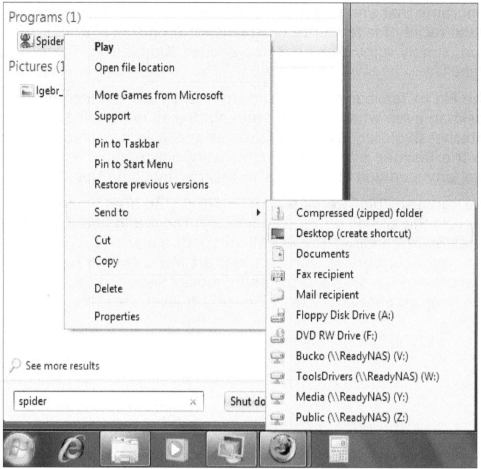

Figure 2.6 – Creating a shortcut on the desktop

You can also drag and drop icons from the Start Menu on to the desktop but doing so may remove them from your Start Menu, which is probably not what you want.

We have covered a lot of new material in this chapter, if you are new to computers you might be feeling a little overwhelmed. In that case, master the basic skills of launching programs by searching for them first. You don't need to learn how to pin icons to your Taskbar or Start Menu in order to use your computer, these steps are completely optional.

Lesson 3 – Windows In Windows 7

As you might imagine, windows are an important concept to master in Windows 7. Virtually every program you run on a Windows machine will create a window of some kind, the only exception being certain game and multimedia titles which take over the whole screen. Windows 7 comes with some nifty new features for managing windows, which we will delve into in this lesson.

3.1 - A Windows 7 window

The majority of windows you will work with in Windows 7 have a common set of controls at the top. Take a look at figure 3.1 below:-

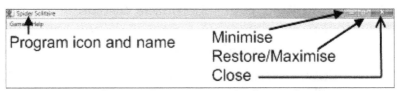

Figure 3.1 – Common window elements

At the left of the window is the programs icon (which you will see on the Taskbar when the program is running) and also the name of the window (which is usually the programs name). Directly below that, programs often have menus which can be accessed by clicking on them. In the picture above you may be able to make out "Game" and "Help".

On the right of the window we have the common window controls. Clicking Minimise hides the window and shrinks the application down to the Taskbar. Unlike previous versions of Windows, items on the Taskbar are now represented by icons. To maximise the window again, click on the programs icon.

Clicking Close will close down the application completely, fairly self explanatory.

The middle button (labelled Restore/Maximise in figure 3.1) changes depending on what state the window is in. When a window is maximised, that is, sized to fill all the available space on your monitor, this button is called "Restore". Clicking on restore will make the window slightly smaller. Why would you want to do this? Simply because it makes it easier to resize and move the window, as we will see in a moment.

If the window is not maximised then clicking on the middle button will maximise it, expanding it to fill up all available space on your desktop.

3.2 - Moving and resizing

When a window is not maximised, it is easy to move and resize it. To move a window, simply click with your left mouse button on the title bar and hold your left mouse button down. Now, drag the window to wherever you want it. When the window is in place, let go of your mouse button.

To resize a window, firstly move your mouse pointer to the edge of the window. When the pointer is in the correct place, it will turn into two oppositely pointing arrows. Click your left mouse button and hold it down, then drag with the mouse and let go. Your window will now snap to the new size. You can resize from any side, and from the corners too, which allows you to adjust the width and height at the same time. Figure 3.2 shows a mouse pointer ready to resize a window:-

Figure 3.2 – When your mouse pointer looks like two arrows, you are ready to resize your window

3.3 - New ways to work with windows

Windows 7 introduces some great new tools to make working with Windows easier and more productive. As you start becoming more confident with your PC, you will start working with more and more open windows at once. Windows 7 introduces some useful new features for managing windows.

Aero Peek:- In lesson 1, we touched on how the Taskbar has been overhauled for Windows 7. Instead of window names, we now get icons. When a program opens multiple windows, the icons stack on top of each other. To help you find the correct window, you can use Aero Peek. Hover your mouse pointer over icons on the Taskbar and you will see a preview of their window. Figure 3.3 illustrates this:-

Figure 3.3 – Using Aero Peek to preview windows from the Taskbar

To open one of the windows you are peeking at, simply click on the preview with your mouse. You can also hover your mouse pointer over the preview icon and see a full screen preview of the window. This will temporarily turn all the other windows transparent so you can focus on the window you are previewing.

Aero Peek works with Internet Explorer too. If you use tabbed browsing (we cover this in lesson 35.2), you will see previews of your open tabs. This doesn't work in some third party browsers yet, but it won't be long before they catch up. Aero Peek only works if your Windows 7 machine is running the Aero Glass desktop.

Aero Snap:- If you are used to working with multiple windows, you will know that windows can often become cluttered on your desktop. Windows 7 gives you a great new tool to help with this called Aero Snap. Take any window and then move it off to the edge of your screen on either side, you will then see a transparent frame appear. Let go of the mouse button now and the window will snap to exactly half of the screen width.

Aero Shake:- Aero Shake is a new Windows 7 feature possibly born out of frustration. If you are working with a desktop with a lot of open windows, all piled on top of one another in a chaotic fashion, simply grab the window you want to work with from the chaos and then by holding down your mouse button (just like when you move a window) shake it quite vigorously. Now the other windows on your desktop are minimised and you will be left with just the window you were shaking. You can also shake the window again to reverse the effect.

Aero flip:- Just like in Windows Vista, you can hold down the Windows key on your keyboard and press Tab to cycle through open windows in 3D. Keep pressing tab to cycle through the windows.

So, hopefully you will have discovered that working with windows in Windows 7 is easy and dare we say even fun? That is the end of the first chapter, in the next chapter we will start exploring the folders and files on your computer and discover how to work with multimedia content.

Chapter 2 – Working With Files

Computers run programs that manipulate information. In our ultra connected internet age, desktop and laptop computers in homes crunch through data and information at a rate that would have humbled the supercomputers of the past. Never before has it been easier and quicker to manipulate your pictures, videos and music files. In this chapter, we will show you how you can work with files and folders on your computer. The program you will be using to do this is called Windows Explorer. Windows Explorer makes working with files as easy as organising a filing cabinet, easier in fact, since it does all the lifting and refiling for you!

Lesson 4 – Personal Folders

You may remember we briefly mentioned user accounts and personal folders in our previous lessons. In this lesson, we will start to explore personal folders on a Windows 7 machine.

4.1 - Your personal folders

Your personal folder is where most of your pictures, videos, documents and other files will be stored by default. To access it, open the Start Menu and then click on your account name at the top. See figure 4.1 for an example:-

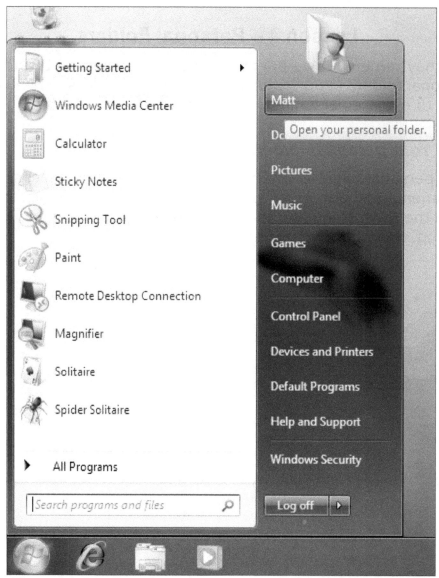

Figure 4.1 – Opening your personal Documents folder

A typical personal folder will open in Windows Explorer and look something like figure 4.2:-

Figure 4.2 – A typical personal folder for a Windows 7 user

In figure 4.2 you can see several sub-folders, including a downloads folder. The downloads folder stores files that you download from the web. The "My Documents", "My Music" "My Pictures" and "My Videos" are provided for storing various multimedia data. These folders should be familiar to those of you who have used Windows before. There is also a folder called "Saved Games", which is intended for storing saved game data (such as high scores or last level reached). The "Searches" folder is for saved searches. If you regularly search for a certain type of document on your PC, you can save the search criteria in that folder for quick reference.

To open folders in Windows Explorer, we double click on them. So to see the contents of "My Pictures" for example, we simply double click on it.

When we view files and folders on a Windows 7 machine, we

use Windows Explorer. Figure 4.2 shows a Windows Explorer window that is viewing our personal documents folder. We will take a more in-depth look at Windows Explorer in figure 4.3:-

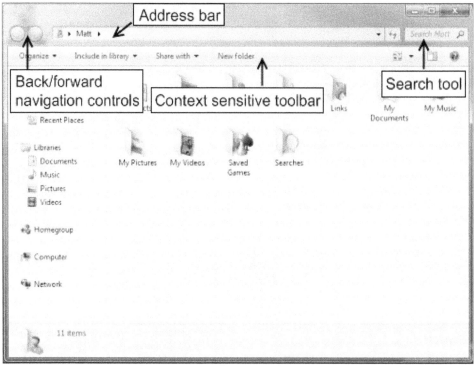

Figure 4.3 – Elements of a Windows Explorer window

4.2 - The individual elements of a Windows Explorer window

Back/forward navigation controls:- As you browse through folders, you can use the back button (the arrow pointing to the left) to go back to the folder you were previously viewing. Similarly, the forward button (the arrow pointing to the right) will take you forward again.

Address bar:- The Address bar shows the address of the file on your computer. This is often referred to as the file path. Expert users can even type the address or path of a file directly into the address bar.

Search tool:- If you need to search through the contents of a folder, enter your search query here. Note that searching like this will only search through the contents of the current folder and its sub-folders, not through the entire computer.

Context sensitive toolbar:- The actions on this toolbar change depending on the type of file or folder we are working with. For example, on the "My Music" folder, the toolbar will change to display actions relevant for working with and listening to music files. When you click on an individual file or folder the toolbar may change again.

4.3 - Breadcrumbs

If you want to find your way back along a path, then leaving a trail of breadcrumbs might work, provided there's nothing around to eat them. Since birds and other animals don't eat digital breadcrumbs, you can rely on them for finding your way back down the path and off in other directions. Take a look at figure 4.4, it shows an example of using the breadcrumbs feature to navigate around folders:-

Figure 4.4 – Using breadcrumbs to navigate around folders in the path

In figure 4.4 we have opened the breadcrumbs menu at "Matt". This is the personal folder that we had opened in figure 4.3. The menu is showing us all the other folders we could navigate to from there. Rather than having to navigate back to the folder we can simply use the breadcrumbs here to quickly jump off to somewhere else.

Breadcrumbs are an advanced user feature so don't worry if you don't quite understand them yet. Do not be afraid to experiment for yourself, it is not possible to break anything playing with this feature.

4.4 - Folder views

Computers view all data as strings of binary numbers, but people are much more visual than that. Fortunately, there are several ways we can represent content in Windows Explorer. Refer to figure 4.5 for a list of all the different folder view

modes:-

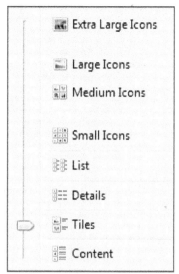

Figure 4.5 – Folder viewing modes

So what do all those viewing options do? Take a look at the following pictures for an example. These screenshots were taken from within a picture folder, other content will look different, of course.

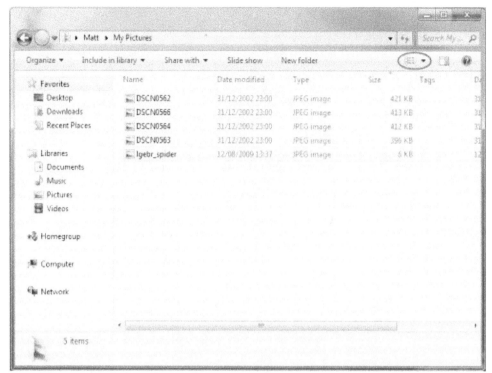

Figure 4.6.1 – Details view, the power users favourite

Details view is used most often when working with large numbers of files. You can easily see important information such as file types and sizes. In all viewing modes, you can click the icon circled in figure 4.6.1 to change the view mode or click the downward pointing arrow to access the view mode menu shown in figure 4.5.

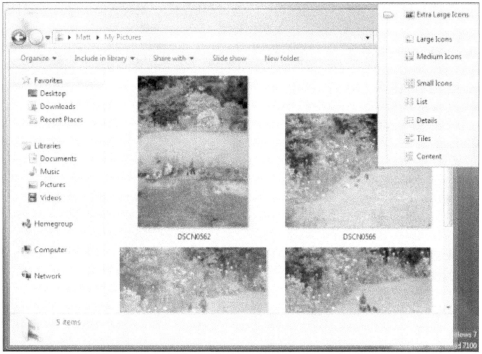

Figure 4.6.2 – Extra large icons view

An icon is a visual representation of a file or folder on your computer. In Windows Explorer under Windows 7, we can choose four different sizes of icon. Picture files will show a thumb nail preview as seen in figure 4.6.2 if the icon size is large enough.

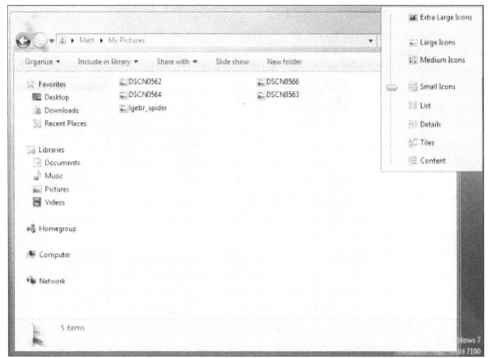

Figure 4.6.3 – Small icons view

In small icons view, the icons become too small to show a thumbnail picture preview and so simply revert to this small representation of a picture.

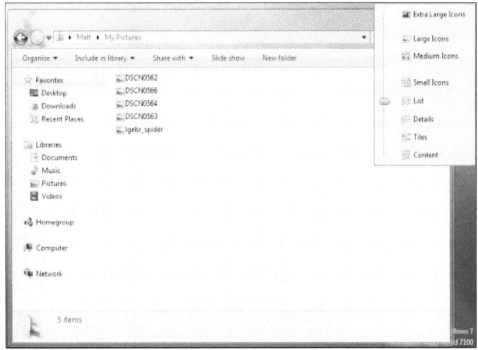

Figure 4.6.4 – List view

List view is similar to Details view except without quite as many details.

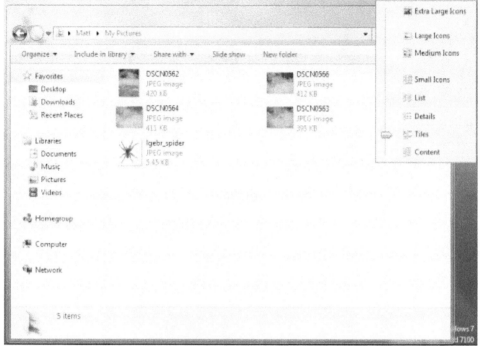

Figure 4.6.5 – Tiles view

Tiles view is similar to Medium Icons view except some information about the files is placed on the right next to the icon.

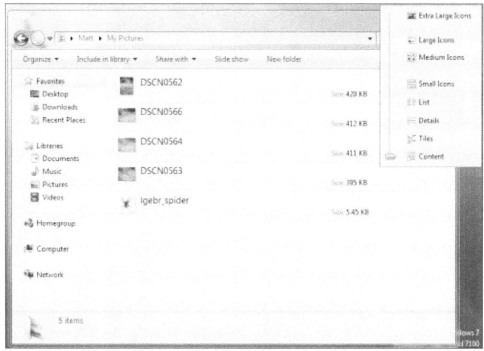

Figure 4.6.6 – Content view

Content view aims to strike a balance between Details view and Icon view. Files are arranged in a list with their file sizes shown on the right.

4.5 - Delving into Details view

Details view lets you find out all kinds of information about files on your computer. In figure 4.6.1, we can see the date that the files were modified, what type of file they are, their sizes and any tags that are applied (we cover tags in lesson 15.1). Right clicking on a column heading in Details view enables us to add a new column, figure 4.7 demonstrates this:-

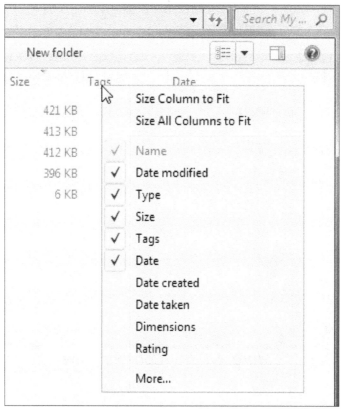

Figure 4.7 – Customizing Details view by adding more columns of information

After right clicking on a column heading, adding or removing new columns is just a matter of clicking on them. By clicking on "More..." at the bottom of the menu you can choose from hundreds of different types of meta-data (data about data). Not all meta-data is relevant to all kinds of files, for example a picture of your back garden isn't usually going to have an "Album Artist" and your favourite music file is unlikely to have "Dimensions", at least not the kind that can be measured in inches or centimetres.

You can also sort your list of files by any of the columns you currently have displayed in Details view. Simply click on the column to sort by that criteria, click again on the same column to reverse the sorting order (i.e change from sorting from high to low or A to Z to low to high or Z to A).

4.6 - Preview pane

When you want to open a file in Windows Explorer, you double click on it. If you are sifting through a lot of files at once however, you might find it more convenient to use the preview pane. Figure 4.8 shows the preview pane opened, the icon circled is the icon you will need to click to open the preview pane.

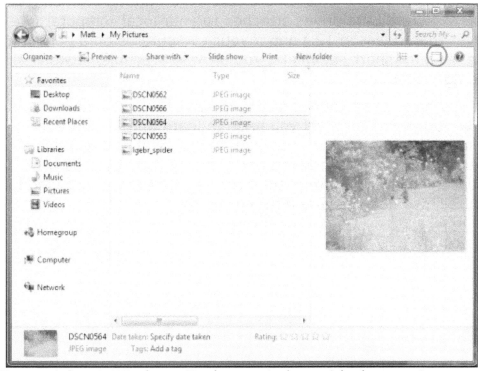

Figure 4.8 – A Windows Explorer window with the preview pane enabled. Notice how the selected file appears in the preview on the right

4.7 - Navigation pane

The navigation pane is the list of items on the left hand side of the Windows Explorer window. You can see it clearly in all the previous screen shots. If you find you are often using the same folder, you can add it to your Favorites. Right click on "Favorites" next to the little star icon at the top and then choose "Add current location to Favorites".

The other short-cuts in the navigation pane will take you to various places which we will be covering in later lessons. The "Libraries" folders we cover in lesson 7. The Homegroup folders are shared folders on your network. Homegroups are covered in lesson 36. There are also short-cuts to "Computer", which lets you explore all the drives attached to your local computer (we cover that in lesson 12) and if your computer is on a network, the network short-cut will let you browse available network storage locations.

As you have seen, there are lots of ways to work with your data in Windows 7. Don't feel you have to learn and master every possible way to display your data, experiment and use the views that work best for you and the way you work. As with most things in computing, the best way to learn is by trying for yourself, so don't be afraid to have a go.

Lesson 5 – Working With Folders

In this lesson we will be building on some of the skills we developed in the previous lesson by taking a more detailed look at folders and files. For those of you who have used Windows before, much of the material here may be familiar. If this is your first time using Windows then, as always, we encourage you to learn at your own pace and experiment when reviewing the material presented here.

5.1 - Opening folders

Figure 4.2 in the previous lesson showed a Windows Explorer window open at our personal folder. Figure 5.1 below shows the same thing:-

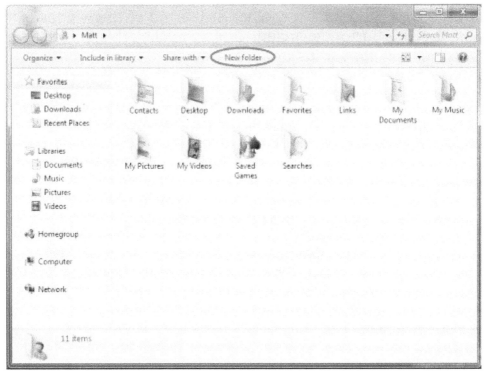

Figure 5.1 – Windows Explorer open on a users personal folder

Although the folders you can see in the picture are named "My Documents" "My Music", "My Videos" and so on, you can still copy any kind of information into these folders and that holds true for all folders on a Windows PC. Opening any folder is as simple as double clicking on it.

5.2 - Making your own folders

Just like with a real world filing cabinet, you can create your own folders inside your computer too. Unlike a typical office filing cabinet however, on your Windows 7 PC you can create a new folder wherever you like (except in protected locations such as operating system folders). You can nest new folders inside another folder, and folders inside these folders too. In fact you can nest folders almost without limits. You can create a new folder in several ways, the easiest is to simply click "New folder" from the context sensitive toolbar at the top of the window. In figure 5.1 this button is circled. Once you click this button, the new folder will appear instantly, all you need to do is type in a name for the folder using the keyboard.

Creating folders is great for organising files on your computer. You can create sub-folders for different projects, different events that you photographed or filmed perhaps, different albums or artists in your music collection or any way you choose.

5.3 - The context menu in Windows Explorer

We briefly saw the context menu in lesson 1 when we were exploring the Start Menu. The context menu is very handy when working with files too. To open the context menu in Windows Explorer, simply right click on a file or folder. Figure 5.2 shows the resulting menu:-

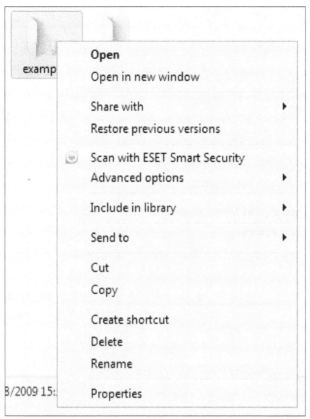

Figure 5.2 – Right click on a file or folder to open a context menu containing some common tasks associated with files and folders

Context menus vary slightly between machines, for example we have the ESET Smart Security package installed on this machine, which has added some extra entries to our context menu. Most of the options you can see in figure 5.2 will be covered in later lessons. In this lesson we will show you some of the most common tasks you can perform with files and folders from the context menu.

5.4 - Send to

Hovering your mouse pointer over the "Send to" option opens

up another sub-menu. Figure 5.3 shows this menu:-

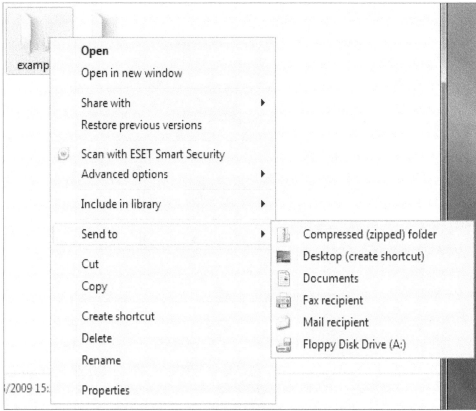

Figure 5.3 – The Send to menu

From this menu we can send the file or folder to various places or programs on our PC. What do each of these options do? We will take a look at each one now.

Compressed (zipped) folder:- This option creates a zip file with the files and folders we currently have selected. You can think of a zipped folder as being a compressed collection of files and folders. If you have dozens of files you want to transport across the internet, compressing them into a zipped folder can make them much easier to manage. Note that sending files or folders to a compressed (zipped) folder will not damage them in any way, nor will it remove them from their original locations. Accessing files inside a compressed or zipped folder is slower than accessing them in a normal folder.

Desktop (create shortcut):- This creates a shortcut to the file or folder on our desktop. The shortcut icon will appear on the same area as the Recycle Bin icon.

Documents:- Sends the currently selected file or folder to our documents folder. If the file or folder is already in our documents folder, it will create a copy.

Fax recipient:- Sends the currently selected document or folder to the Fax machine. This option will only work correctly if you have configured your Fax or Fax/Modem correctly. See the documentation that accompanied your hardware for more information.

Mail recipient:- Sends the currently selected files or folders to your e-mail program where they can then be forwarded across the internet to friends or associates. This option will only work if you have configured desktop e-mail software correctly. Avoid sending excessive or large files through e-mail as this may cause problems with many popular e-mail services.

Floppy Disk Drive:- If your computer still has an old fashioned floppy disk drive, choosing this option will copy the files (space permitting) to the floppy disk in drive A. It is a little surprising to see the venerable floppy disk still featured on the send to menu in these days of gigabyte sized USB drives physically no bigger than your thumb!

5.5 - Cut, copy and paste

Directly below the Send to options are the Cut and Copy options. Mastering the art of cut, copy and paste is one of the best things you can do to make yourself more productive on your Windows PC. Cut is used for moving files or folders, whereas copy is used (unsurprisingly) to copy them. Take a look at figure 5.4:-

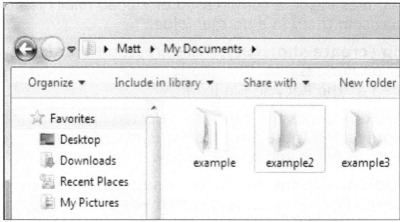

Figure 5.4 – Folders in a Windows Explorer window

If you wanted to move the folder named "example2", shown in figure 5.4 so that it was nested inside the folder named "example", you could do this by using the context menu. Right click on the "example2" folder and choose "Cut" from the context menu. Now, open the folder you want to move the file or folder into, in this case the folder called "example". Now right click on an empty space in the Windows Explorer window and choose "Paste" from the context menu. The "example2" folder will then appear. If we had chosen "Copy" instead of "Cut" then the folder would not have been removed from its original location.

You can also move files and folders by dragging them. Dragging is done by clicking with your left mouse button on an icon and then holding down your left button. Now, as you move your mouse the icon will move too. You can now simply drop the icon wherever you want it to move. We explore this in more detail in lesson 6.1.

5.6 - *When file names collide*

Windows needs to tell files apart just the same as you do, so you cannot have two files with the same name in the same folder.

If you try and put a file with the same name as an existing one into the same folder, Windows will show you information about both files and ask you to confirm that you want to replace the original file.

If you try and put a folder with the same name as an existing one into the same folder, the contents of the folders will be merged. Any files which exist inside both folders will be overwritten. If a file is in the source folder but not in the destination folder, it will be moved to the destination. If a file is in the destination folder but not the source folder, it will be left alone. Figure 5.5 shows two folders. Notice how there's a file called "File3.txt" in both folders.

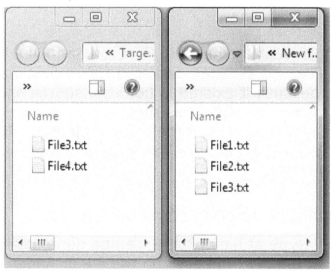

Figure 5.5 – Two folders prior to being merged

Now, consider figure 5.6, here the contents of the two folders have been merged together:-

Figure 5.6 – The merged contents of two folders, shading has been added to two of the files for illustration purposes

In the example illustrated above, File1.txt and File2.txt are unchanged. File3.txt (shaded darker in figure 5.6) was overwritten, because it existed in both the source and the destination folders. File4.txt was moved in from its original location, because it existed in the source folder but NOT in the destination. We will explore file name collisions more in lesson 6.2.

5.7 - Renaming or deleting files and folders

Renaming any type of file or folder can be done easily from the context menu. Simply right click on the file or folder you want to work with then choose "Rename" from the context menu. Now, type a new name and press Enter.

Eventually you will want to remove a file or folder from your PC.

You can do this easily from the context menu, simply right click on a file and choose "Delete". Windows will ask you to confirm that you definitely want to remove the file or folder. Click on "Yes" and it will be removed. Files and folders that are deleted are usually (but not always) sent to the Recycle Bin. You should see the Recycle Bin on your desktop, you can open it with a double click. To take a file out of the Recycle Bin, right click on it and choose "Restore". We take a more detailed look at the Recycle Bin in lesson 10.

You can also delete files or folders by clicking on them once and then pressing the Delete key on your keyboard.

That concludes this lesson. By now you are becoming quite competent at working with files and folders on your PC, the next lesson will show you some advanced techniques for dealing with large numbers of files. Remember, practise makes perfect so don't be afraid to try out the techniques we have reviewed here.

Lesson 6 – Working With Multiple Files And Folders

In the last lesson, we saw how to use the context menu to copy and move files on our hard drive. In this lesson, we will review and build on those skills as we work with multiple files.

6.1 - Dragging and dropping

This is a somewhat difficult concept to explain with just words and pictures. You can move, or drag an icon by clicking on it with your left mouse button. Then, keeping your mouse button held down, move your mouse. The file or folder will now follow your mouse cursor. Figure 6.1 shows an example of a folder being dragged into another folder:-

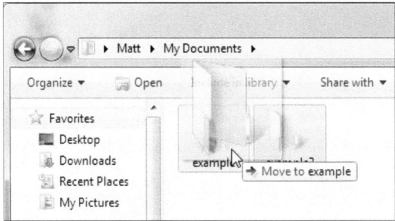

Figure 6.1 – Dragging a folder into another folder will move it

6.2 - File name collisions revisited

We already learned that we can't have two files or folders with the same name in the same folder. If there is a file name collision when copying or moving a folder, you'll see the following window appear:-

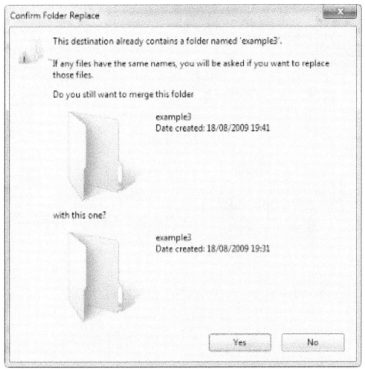

*Figure 6.2 – Windows needs your permission to merge these
two folders*

The choice is pretty easy here, click on "Yes" to merge the
folders or "No" to abort the operation. If you click on "Yes" the
folders will be merged, see lesson 5.6 for an example of a
merged folder.

If there is a file name collision during the folder merge, you will
then see the window shown in figure 6.3:-

Figure 6.3 – A file collision when merging a folder

You now have three options to resolve the conflict:-

Copy and replace:- Copies the new file over the top of the old one, the old file will not be recoverable.

Don't copy:- Leaves the old file in place and does not move or copy the new file.

Copy, but keep both files:- Renames the new file so that both files can exist in the same folder.

Notice how Windows gives us information about when the file was last modified, you can use this information to determine which is the most recent copy of a document. Be cautious however, if you copy and replace a file, it is not easy to recover the old file without special software.

6.3 - Aero Snap and multiple Windows Explorer windows

It is possible to drag and drop files between Windows Explorer windows. A neat way of setting this up is to use Aero Snap. When working, copying and moving files between two folders, you can use Aero snap to size Windows Explorer windows to exactly half the screen width. To do this, you need to drag the window to the edge of the screen until a transparent frame appears (remember, to drag a window you click and hold on its title bar as you move your mouse). See figure 6.4 for an example:-

Figure 6.4 – Using Aero Snap to resize a Windows Explorer window, wait for the transparent box to appear before letting go of the mouse button

Once you have snapped one window to one side of the screen, repeat the process with the other window. If you don't have another Windows Explorer window, the easiest way to open one is to right click on the folder you want to work with and choose "Open in new window". Figure 6.5 shows this:-

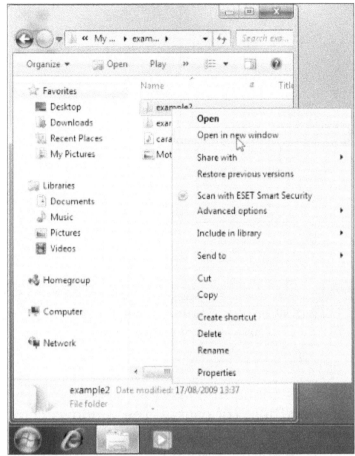

Figure 6.5 – Right click on a folder and choose "Open in new window" to open up a whole new Windows Explorer window

Now you can drag the new window to the other side of the screen and use Aero Snap to snap it into position. Figure 6.6 shows a screen shot of a desktop configured like this:-

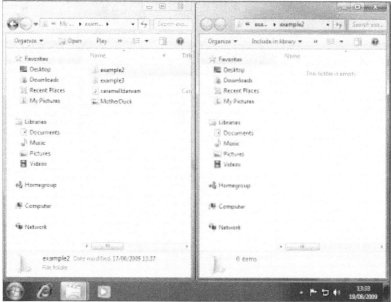

Figure 6.6 – Two Windows Explorer windows 'Aero Snapped' to the sides of the screen

With your windows configured like this, it is easy to drag and drop files between them (of course, the windows could be sized or positioned however you like, but this configuration is particularly convenient for working with two folders at once).

To move files between the two folders, all you need to do is drag the file across from one window to the other. Files can be moved back in exactly the same way.

Remember when using this technique that dragging a file from one window to another can either move or copy the file, depending on the storage device you are working with. Files are moved if you drag them between two folders on the same storage device. If you drag a file or folder from one storage device to another, the files are copied instead.

To demonstrate this, consider an external USB stick/thumb drive. USB stick drives (also known as thumb drives or pen drives) are portable storage devices which can be attached to the common USB connectors on most modern computers. They are very useful for transporting files to and from work, school or college, for example. When we drag a file from our computers hard drive onto a device like this, it is copied, rather than moved. Why is this? It is not usually worth making lots of copies of a file over the same drive since it just wastes space. When you are working with a removable drive on the other hand, perhaps for backup or transporting files, it would not be a good idea to remove the originals from your computer, especially considering how easy it is to lose a USB stick drive!

6.4 - Working with multiple files at once

So far we have been working with individual files and folders, but what if we wanted to copy or move dozens of files at once? Fortunately for us, we do not have to do them one at a time. There are several ways we can select more than one file or folder at once. One of the easiest ways is to lasso them. To do this, click in an empty space in the Windows Explorer window and hold down your mouse button, just like you do when you drag an icon or window. You will see a square start to appear, Figure 6.7 illustrates this:-

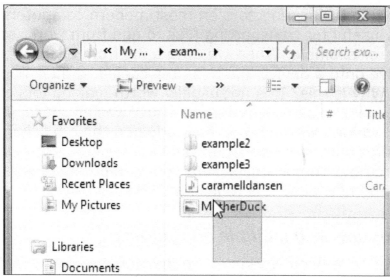

Figure 6.7 – Creating a lasso rectangle by dragging the mouse

Drag the lasso rectangle over the files you want to select and then let go. Now all of the files that were within the boundary of the lasso will be selected.

6.5 - Keyboard short cuts for working with multiple files

There are also some handy keyboard short cuts for selecting multiple files:-

Shift The Shift key (sometimes represented as a small up pointing arrow) is located at the far right and far left of the second row of keys from the bottom on a standard keyboard. Using Shift, you can select a range of files from a list. For example, to select the two folders and the first file in figure 6.7, first click on the "example2" folder, then hold down shift and click on the "caramelldansen" file.

Ctrl The Control or Ctrl key is located at the far right and far left of the bottom row of keys on a standard keyboard. This key can be used to select and deselect individual files. Simply hold down Control while you click on files and folders to individually select and deselect them. Any files you click while holding down Control will stay selected.

When you have multiple files selected, you can work with them just like you do with an individual file. That means you can use the context menu to Cut, Copy or Send to, or you can drag and drop them. When working with a large number of files, selecting several at once is a huge time-saver, so be sure to practise and master this technique.

That concludes this lesson. Now you have a solid understanding of how to manipulate files on your computer.

In the next lesson we look at Libraries, a new Windows 7 feature that helps you organise your data.

Lesson 7 – Libraries

Modern computer users are storing more and more information on their machines. Digital cameras have made it super easy to take thousands of pictures. The internet has made it cheap and easy to purchase huge music collections and even video collections too. Libraries are a new feature introduced in Windows 7 to help manage users rapidly expanding file collections. Power users are already raving about Libraries, but regular users often find them confusing.

7.1 - Working with Libraries

Libraries appear just like folders when you are working with them in Windows Explorer, but in actual fact they can show data from several locations on your computer. This can be useful if you want to browse all your photographs or music together, for example. Figure 7.1 shows the Music library on a Windows 7 machine.

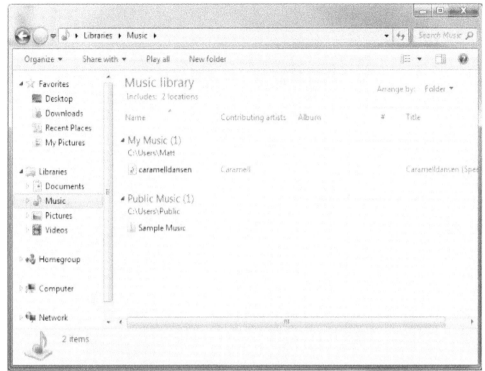

Figure 7.1 – Windows Explorer in the Music library on a Windows 7 machine. Note how two locations are included.

In the library folder shown in figure 7.1, what we are actually seeing is a combined view of My Music folder and the Public Music folder. So in effect this library is showing us the content in both of these folders. Notice that the "2 locations" text in figure 7.1 is blue when shown on screen, if we click on this text we can see which locations are included in our library. Figure 7.2 illustrates this:-

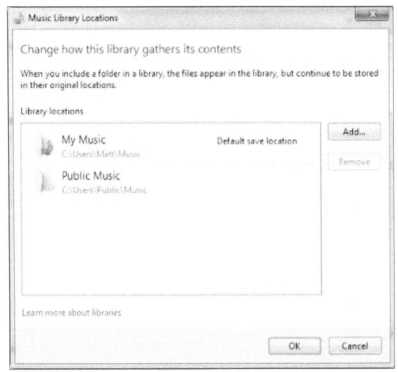

Figure 7.2 – The contents of the Music library is made up of these two folders

Notice in figure 7.2 that "My Music" is marked as the "Default save location". What does this mean? Since we can work with our libraries like any other folder, if we were to copy or move a file into this library from somewhere else, the file would actually be placed into the My Music folder.

It is also possible to add other locations to a library, such as a network storage device or even a removable hard drive. There are some restrictions on what kind of drives can be added to Libraries. Unfortunately, USB thumb or stick drives are not supported and you can only add network locations that are indexed and available off-line (this basically means their contents are mirrored on your computers hard drive). For more information about what files and folders can be included, click on the "Learn more about libraries" link at the bottom of the window and then click "What types of locations are supported in libraries?".

If you want to add a location to your library, simply click on "Add..." and then browse to the folder you want to include. Once you have done this, the contents of that folder will appear in the library.

7.2 - Sorting data in libraries

When working with libraries in Windows Explorer, they behave almost exactly the same as regular folders. Figure 7.3 shows a typical Music library with several folders added to it:-

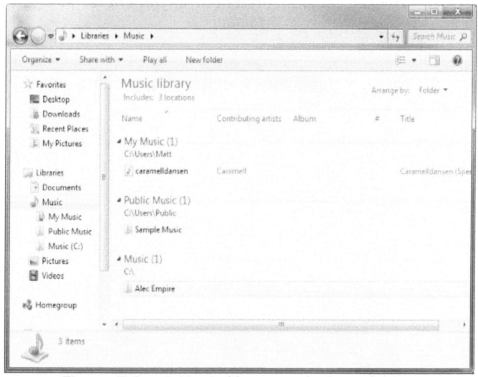

Figure 7.3 – A Music library with three folders

By default, the information is arranged by folder, but we can arrange it in different ways (depending on the type of content) by clicking on the blue text next to "Arrange by:". Figure 7.4 shows this:-

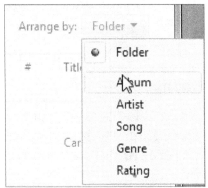

Figure 7.4 – Choosing a different arrangement for a library folder

Figure 7.5 shows a Music library arranged by album:-

Figure 7.5 – A Music library arranged by album

In figure 7.5 above we can see several albums in the library. We can listen to an album by right clicking on the icon and choosing "Play with Windows Media Player" from the context menu. If you have used Windows Media Player before you will know that it has a built in library for your music. In Windows 7 the Music library here and in Windows Media player is linked. Any music you copy into your Music library here will also be added to the Windows Media Player Music library.

Don't forget that you can also use the folder views control to change how data is arranged in your libraries, just like we did with regular folders in lesson 4.4.

7.3 - Pictures library

The Pictures library behaves in much the same way as the Music library. Figure 7.6 shows a typical Pictures library:-

Figure 7.6 – A Pictures library

There are two locations included by default in a standard Windows 7 Pictures library, your personal pictures folder and the public pictures folder. In a Pictures library we can arrange the data by Month, Day, Rating or Tag. We will show you how to edit this meta-data in lesson 15.1. Of course, we can also use the folder views and preview pane just like we did with regular folders in lesson 4.

That concludes our lesson on Libraries. Libraries are a great new feature of Windows 7, as time goes by more and more applications will take advantage of them just like Windows

Media Player does, helping to reduce searching times and duplicate files on your PC.

Chapter 3 – Deeper Into Folders

In this chapter we will continue to build your Windows 7 skills by looking at some advanced folder and file operations. You have come a long way since the start of the course and you are rapidly turning into a Windows 7 expert! Remember, read, watch and review the material at your own pace. As we delve into these more complex subjects you might find you need to refresh your memory from earlier chapters. Learning to use an operating system well is not a race, so take your time.

Lesson 8 – Folder Properties

Folders on a Windows 7 machine have unique attributes, or properties associated with them. In this lesson we will delve into these properties and explore some of the attributes we can change.

8.1 - Accessing folder properties

To access the folder properties for any given folder, simply right click on the folder and choose "Properties" from down at the bottom of the context menu. Figure 8.1 illustrates this:-

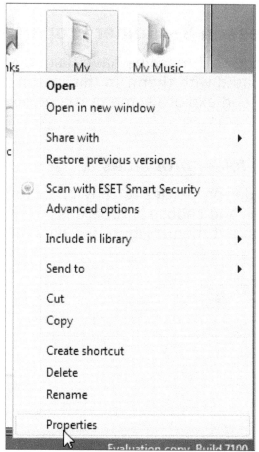

Figure 8.1 – Accessing folder properties

Once you do this, you will see the Folder Properties window open, figure 8.2 shows this window:-

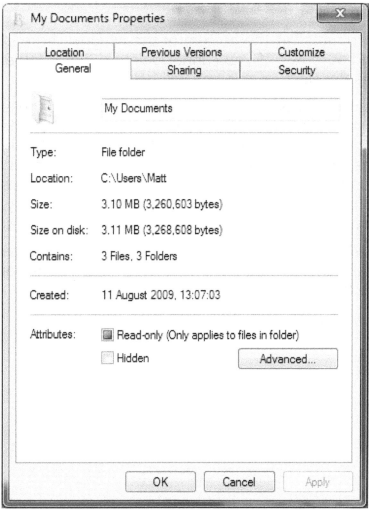

Figure 8.2 – The Properties window for the "My Documents" folder

By default the Folder Properties window will open on the "General" tab. This tab shows us some general information about the folder, such as the size it takes up and how many files it contains. Notice that we can see values for "Size" and "Size on disk". "Size" refers to the total size of all the files, "Size on disk" is the actual amount of storage space these files take up. Size on disk is always a little bigger due to the way files are stored on a hard drive.

Under "Attributes" at the bottom of the window there is a box labelled "Read-only". If you cannot delete a file or folder then sometimes deselecting this box will help.

Notice the tabs labelled "Sharing" and "Security". These tabs let you set permissions for other users to access your folders either locally or over the network (the local network not the internet). We discuss Homegroups and how to share folders on a home network using Homegroups in lesson 36. Discussing security permissions is an advanced topic that you will probably never have to deal with unless you are a systems administrator.

Special folders such as "My Pictures" and "My Music" have a location tab. These folders are actually links to other folders. See figure 8.3:-

Figure 8.3 – Some special folders are actually links to other folders

In figure 8.3 we can see that actually, my personal folder points to "C:\users\matt\documents". The default location should be suitable for most users, but if necessary it is possible to change the location of your personal folder clicking on "Move...". This is occasionally useful if you want to move your pictures or music folder to a larger, secondary hard drive for example.

8.2 - Customize tab

The bulk of this lesson will focus on the options available in this tab. Figure 8.4 below shows the folder Properties window open on the Customize tab:-

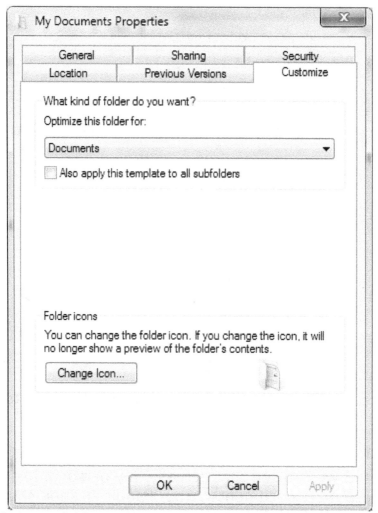

Figure 8.4 – A folder Properties window open on the Customize tab

At the top of the window, we are asked "What kind of folder do you want?" Windows 7 knows about several different types of content and the makers of Windows 7 realised that the best way to view pictures in a folder might not necessarily be the best way to view music, for example. Use the drop down box under "Optimize this folder for:" to tell Windows what type of content is stored in the folder. We can choose from "General Items", "Documents", "Pictures", "Music" and "Videos". When you choose one, Windows will open this folder in a viewing mode suitable for that kind of content.

In lesson 4.4 we demonstrated the different folder viewing modes. It is possible to specify what kind of folder view is used for each type of content. For example, you can have large icons view for pictures and details view for documents, we will show you how in the next lesson.

If the box labelled "Also apply this template to all subfolders" is selected, then any folders inside the current folder will also be switched to documents view, or whatever view was selected in the drop down box.

8.3 - Folder pictures and folder icons

In the bottom of the window shown in figure 8.4 is a button labelled "Change Icon...". Using this option we can change the icon for the folder to any icon we choose. Regular folders that you create yourself (just like we did in lesson 5.2) can be customized even further. Figure 8.5 shows the Customize tab from a user created folder:-

Figure 8.5 – The Customize tab on a user created folder, note that we now have the ability to choose folder pictures too.

You can use any picture on your PC as the folder picture. Click on "Choose File" and then browse to your picture. Choose the picture by clicking on it and then click "Open". Back on the folder properties window, click "Apply". The picture will then be added to the folder in Windows Explorer. If you don't see the picture right away, click on the refresh button (the two arrows pointing up and down next to the address bar in Windows Explorer).

New folder

Figure 8.6 – A folder with a custom picture applied to it

Changing folder icons is also easy. Click on the "Change Icon..." button as shown in figure 8.5. The standard Windows icon library will then appear, this is shown in figure 8.7:-

Figure 8.7 – Browsing for an icon

Browse through the icon gallery here and pick out any icon you like, then click "OK". This will return you to the Folder Properties window. Click on "Apply". You should now see your new icon in

Windows Explorer, if you do not, click on Refresh.

If you want to remove your custom icon, simply access the icon gallery and click the "Restore Defaults" button that can be seen in figure 8.7. To remove a custom folder picture, access the Customize tab of the Folder Properties window (figure 8.5) and click on "Restore Default" under "Folder pictures".

That concludes this lesson on folder properties. Changing and customizing your folders can be useful and fun. Go ahead and experiment for yourself, you can always undo any changes you make by using the "Restore Default" buttons outlined above. In the next lesson we look at advanced folder customization, don't worry, it's not as hard as it sounds!

Lesson 9 – Folder Options

Since we have been exploring folders in the past few lessons, now might be a good time to look at some advanced folder customization options.

9.1 - Folder options window

We can access the folder options window from the Control Panel or, more conveniently from a Windows Explorer window by selecting the Organize menu and then choosing "Folder and search options". Figure 9.1 illustrates this:-

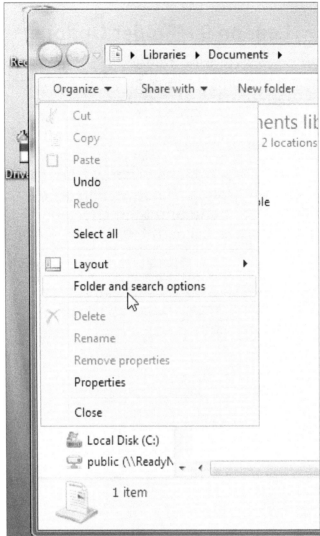

Figure 9.1 – Accessing Folder and search options from Windows Explorer

Figure 9.2 shows the Folder Options window which appears when you select "Folder and search options":-

Figure 9.2 – The Folder Options window

9.2 - The Menu bar

If you have used Windows before, you may notice that this window has not changed very much from Windows Vista or Windows XP but there is one important difference. In previous versions of Windows there was a set of sub-options called "Tasks". These options would allow you to show the tool bar menus on Windows Explorer windows. You can still enable these menus in Windows 7, though they look a little old fashioned and out of place on the new operating system. To enable the menu bar, open the "Organize" menu (the same menu shown in figure 9.1) and then choose Layout, then click on "Menu bar". Figure 9.3 illustrates this:-

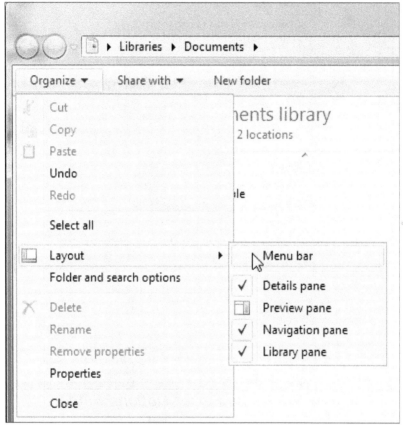

Figure 9.3 – Enabling the Menu bar in Windows Explorer

With the Menu bar enabled, your Windows Explorer windows will have an extra (non context sensitive) menu at the top, figure 9.4 illustrates this:-

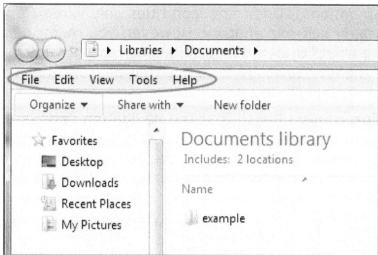

Figure 9.4 – The old fashioned Windows Explorer Menu bar

9.3 - General folder options

Refer back to figure 9.2, there are three categories of options in this window. We will take a look at what each of these options does now.

Browse folders:- In lesson 6 we demonstrated how to work with multiple Windows Explorer windows. We opened a new Windows Explorer window by right clicking on a folder and choosing "Open in new window" in lesson 6.3. By choosing the "Open each folder in its own window" option, you will change the behaviour of Windows Explorer so that every time you double click on a folder, a new Explorer window will open.

With this option enabled, the desktop can become cluttered very quickly, but some users do prefer to work this way.

Click items as follows:- For users who struggle with the timing on double clicks, these options can be very helpful. Choose "Single click to open an item (point to select)" and now you only need to click once on an icon to open it. This does make dragging icons a little more tricky and you may find you accidentally open them when trying to drag, but a lot of users prefer this method rather than the dratted double click.

In the sub options, "Underline icon titles only when I point at them" is fairly self-explanatory. However, you might be wondering what "Underline icon titles consistent with my browser" means. Basically it means that all icon titles (the text below the icons) will be underlined.

Navigation pane:- Recall that the navigation pane is the left hand column on a Windows Explorer window. Choosing the "Show all folders" option changes the layout of the navigation pane so that we can now see our personal folder and the Recycle Bin.

The "Automatically expand to current folder" option is best demonstrated with pictures. Figure 9.5 shows a Windows Explorer window with this option turned off:-

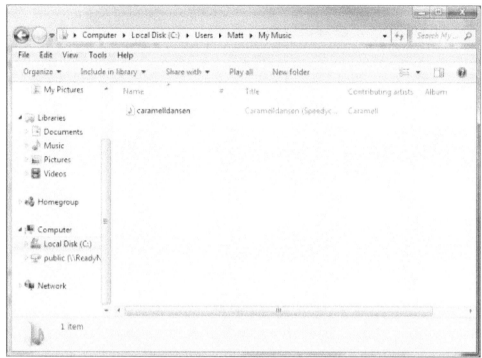

Figure 9.5 – Windows Explorer window with the "Automatically expand to current folder" option turned off

Notice that although the address bar shows that the current folder is "C:\users\Matt\My Music", the navigation pane is still pointing at C:. Now, figure 9.6 shows an Explorer window with the "Automatically expand to current folder" option turned on:-

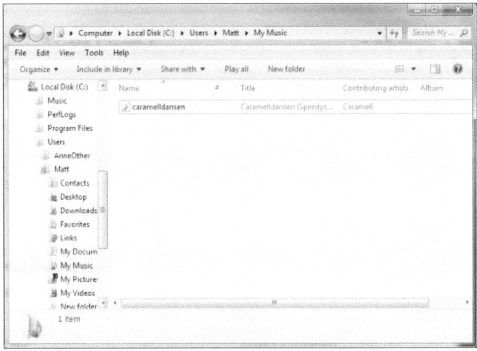

Figure 9.6 - Windows Explorer window with the "Automatically expand to current folder" option turned on

In figure 9.6 you can see that the navigation pane now matches the address or path shown in the address bar. With the Automatically expand to current folder option enabled, the navigation pane will always match the address bar like this.

When changing options in the Folder Options window, don't forget that you can always revert back to the default options by clicking "Restore Defaults" and then clicking on "Apply".

9.4 - View tab

You can access the "View" tab in the Folder Options window by clicking on it once. Figure 9.7 shows the Folder Options window open on the "View" tab:-

Figure 9.7 – The "View" tab of the Folder Options window

There are two main sections to this tab, they are "Folder Views" and "Advanced settings".

The Folder Views options contains just two buttons. By clicking "Apply to folders" it is possible to set the current viewing mode across all folders of the same type. What does this mean? Consider this example, Windows Explorer is viewing a music folder and the viewing mode is set to details view (changing folder viewing modes was covered in lesson 4.4). Now, the user opens the Folder Options window (just like we did at the start of the lesson) and then navigates to the View tab. The user wants all the music folders to open up in details view, so he/she clicks the "Apply to Folders" button. From now on, all music folders will be shown in details view whenever they are opened up.

Clicking on the "Reset Folders" button restores all the folders to their default view.

The Advanced Settings in the bottom half of this tab contain all kinds of tweaks and customizations you can do to Windows Explorer. Rather than try to cover every minor option in excruciating detail, the best way to learn is by experimenting. You cannot damage your computer by changing these options and you can always revert back by clicking on "Restore Defaults".

There are a couple of important options that are found under the advanced options that we do want to look at in detail however:-

9.5 - Hidden files and folders

On a Windows 7 computer, there are several folders that are used exclusively by the operating system. These folders contain files that are used by Windows when it loads and when it runs. Because tampering with these files can potentially be disastrous, by default Windows will hide them from view, so you cannot accidentally navigate into them. Occasionally, while troubleshooting your computer or if directed to do so by a technical support representative, you may need to access these folders. Please be careful if you do modify the contents of these folders however! One mistake and you might find your Windows installation starts acting in a very strange manner or even stops working altogether.

Figure 9.8 shows the root (top level) folder on a Windows 7 hard drive with the "show hidden files, folders and drives" option turned off:-

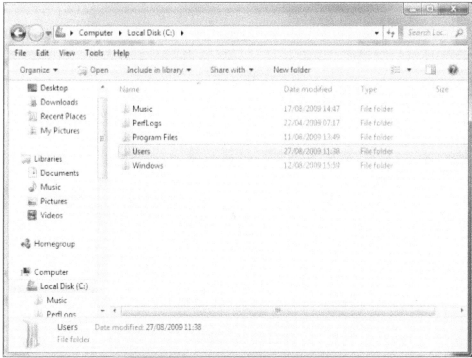

Figure 9.8 – Standard view of the top level directory on a Windows 7 system drive

Figure 9.9 shows the same folder, but with the show hidden files, folders and drives option turned on:-

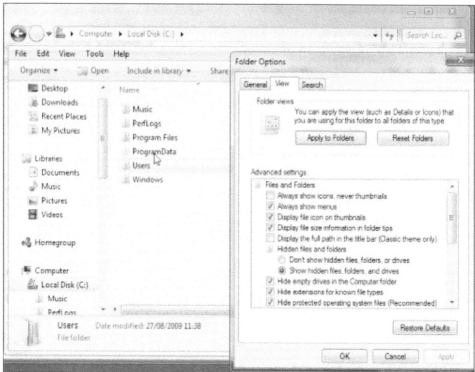

Figure 9.9 – View of the top level directory on a Windows 7 system drive, with the show hidden files, folders and drives option turned on. Notice the extra ProgramData folder under the mouse pointer.

In figure 9.9 we can see an extra folder has appeared (it is directly under the mouse pointer). You may also have noticed that the folder appears fainter, or ghosted compared to the other folders, to indicate that it is normally hidden.

A related option to "Show hidden files, folders and drives" is the "Hide protected operating system files". You can see it in figure 9.9 right at the bottom of the Folder Options window. If you deselect this option, you will see even more files and folders appear on your computer. Again these are important operating system files that you should never change or tamper with unless you are absolutely certain that you know what you are doing. We recommend leaving these files hidden while working normally with your computer.

9.6 - Hide extensions for known file types

This option causes a lot of confusion and even trips up seasoned Windows users. Most files on a Windows computer have a file extension at the end of their file names. A file extension is a period (dot) character followed by three letters or more (historically file extensions were limited to three characters, but in modern versions of Windows they can be longer). Typical file extensions include ".mp3" for mp3 files, ".avi" for video files and ".jpg" for Jpeg photograph files. By default, Windows hides this information from you, this was probably done to make working with files less confusing for beginners.

Refer back to figure 9.5 or 9.6. You can see a music file in Windows Explorer called "Carameldansen". The actual file name of this file is "Carameldansen.mp3" but Windows is hiding the extra file extension information from us. Figure 9.10 shows a Windows Explorer window with the hide file extensions option turned **on** (the default setting).

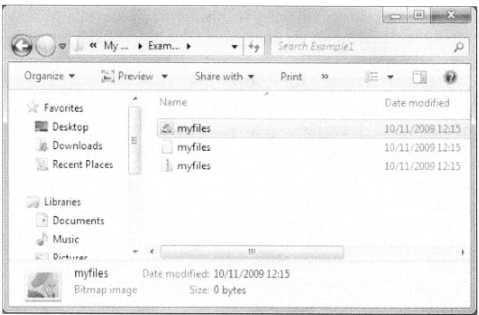

Figure 9.10 – Three files in the same folder with the same name? Not really, the file extensions are different, just Windows is hiding this information from us.

The hide file extensions option can be particularly confusing with files of similar names. In figure 9.10 we have three files. "myfiles.zip", "myfiles.txt" and "myfiles.bmp". With the "Hide extensions for known file types" option turned **on** (the default setting) it appears as if we have three files in the same folder with the same name, something that we already told you is impossible! Figure 9.11 shows the same folder but with the "Hide extensions for known file types" option turned **off**.

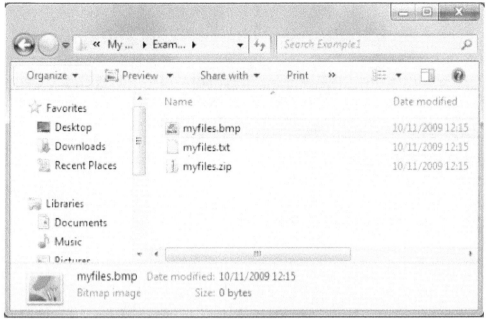

*Figure 9.11 – Turning "Hide extensions for known file types" off
reveals extra information about a file name*

To avoid this kind of confusion, many users turn the "Hide
extensions for known file types" option off. If you do turn it off,
keep in mind that if you rename a file and accidentally remove
its file extension, Windows wont know how to handle that file
any more, unless you rename it again and put the file extension
back. Even worse, if you remove the file extension and put the
wrong one back, Windows may try and open the file with the
wrong program.

That concludes this lesson on folder options. We are getting into
some advanced Windows 7 operations and hope the information
presented here was not too daunting. In the next lesson we will
be looking at the Recycle Bin and how Windows handles the files
you delete.

Lesson 10 – The Recycle Bin

Because it is easy to accidentally delete files and something of a chore to undelete them again, Microsoft introduced the Recycle Bin way back in Windows 95. Now, when you delete files from your PC, they (usually) end up in the Recycle Bin before being removed completely. In this lesson we will explore how the Recycle Bin works and how to recover files that have been sent there.

10.1 - Into the Recycle Bin

Recycle Bin   The Recycle Bin is, by default, the only icon on your Windows 7 desktop. The icon shown here looks as if it has some crumpled paper inside it. This is to indicate that there are files or folders in the bin. To open the Recycle Bin, we simply double click on it. Figure 10.2 shows the Recycle Bin window:-

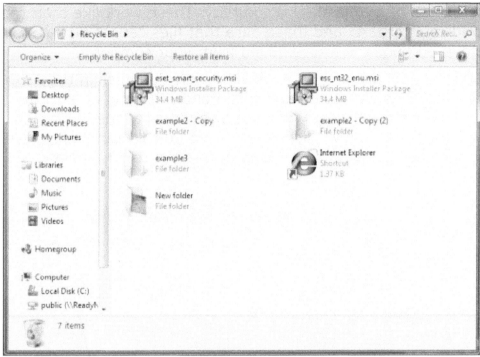

Figure 10.2 – The Recycle Bin opens in a standard Windows Explorer window

The Recycle Bin opens in a Windows Explorer window just like any other folder on your PC. The context menu below the navigation bar has changed to reflect the special tasks that can be carried out with the Recycle Bin. By clicking on "Empty the Recycle Bin", all the items in the window will be permanently deleted. By clicking on "Restore all items", all the items shown are put back into their original folders (i.e the folders that they were placed in before they were deleted).

Notice that we said the files would be "permanently deleted" when "Empty the Recycle Bin" was clicked. This is not strictly true. There is still the possibility of recovering those files with some kind of undelete utility or data forensics tool kit. Emptying the Recycle Bin does not protect you from this. If you are working with particularly sensitive information you may need to use a third party file shredding utility. These work like their real-world counterparts and make sure that files cannot be recovered once the are removed from your computer.

Naturally, it is possible to work with individual files in the Recycle Bin as well as its entire contents. Clicking on a single item reveals the original file path or address at the bottom of the Explorer Window. Clicking on "Restore this item" will move the file back to its original location. See figure 10.3 below:-

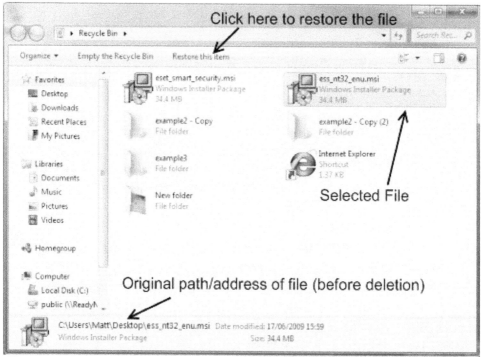

Figure 10.3 – Working with individual files in the Recycle Bin

In figure 10.3, we can see that if we click on "Restore this item", the "ess_nt32_enu.msi" file will be restored to "C:\Users\Matt\Desktop". This is the address or path of the desktop, so the icon would reappear on the desktop in this case.

To permanently delete a selected file, right click on it and choose "Delete" from the context menu.

10.2 - Sending files to the Recycle Bin

Most files that you delete will initially be sent to the Recycle Bin. Take a look at figure 10.4:-

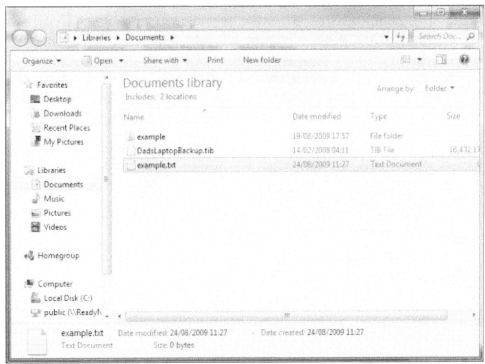

Figure 10.4 – A typical Windows Explorer window

There are several ways to send the file "example.txt" to the Recycle Bin. We can select it and then press the "Delete" key on the keyboard. We can use the "Organize" menu in the top left corner and choose "Delete". Alternatively, use the context menu by right clicking on the icon and then choosing "Delete". Whichever method you prefer, they all have the same end result. Windows will ask us to confirm that we want to delete the file, if we click "Yes", the file is removed from this folder and placed in the Recycle Bin. Once there, we can click on it and see where it came from and then restore it back to its original location if necessary.

10.3 - Files that are not sent to the Recycle Bin

While most files you delete are initially sent to the Recycle Bin, some are not. In figure 10.4 we can see a large file called "DadsLaptopBackup.tib". This file is over 16 gigabytes in size. Files this large are normally just too big to fit in the Recycle Bin. We can still remove them by deleting them with any of the methods described previously. Windows will still prompt us and ask us if we want to send the file to the Recycle Bin, however this time when "Yes" is clicked, the following window will appear:-

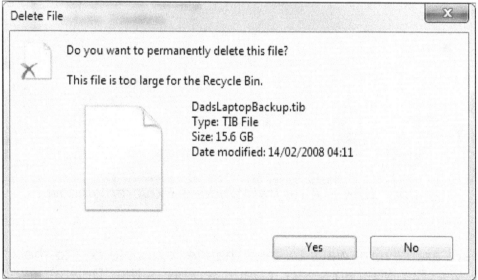

Figure 10.5 – This file is too big to fit in the Recycle Bin

If you click "Yes" then the file will be removed from your computer. Of course, it would still be possible (though somewhat inconvenient) to use special data recovery software to undelete it.

Certain other files are not sent to the Recycle Bin when deleted, to explain why we need to explore some technical information about how the Recycle Bin works.

10.4 - Recycle Bin folders

The Recycle Bin is a little like the library folders in that in actual fact it is an aggregate or combined view of several folders. Each drive on your computer, be it internal or external, can have its own Recycle Bin folder. This folder is normally a hidden folder called "$Recycle.Bin". When you open the Recycle Bin then the folder that opens shows the combined view of all the "$Recycle.Bin" folders on your PC.

If you connect to a storage device, perhaps a network drive or network folder that hasn't had a Recycle Bin configured, then any files that you delete will not be sent to the Recycle Bin they will just be removed. Windows will warn you that the file will be permanently removed so make sure you pay attention to the messages and be extra careful.

So, with those two important exceptions, all files and folders you delete are sent to your Recycle Bin first. Note that you can also empty the Recycle Bin by right clicking on it and choosing "Empty Recycle Bin".

10.5 - Recycle Bin Properties

There are some advanced Recycle Bin preferences that can be changed by right clicking on the Recycle Bin and choosing "Properties". Figure 10.6 shows the Recycle Bin Properties window:-

Figure 10.6 – A Recycle Bin Properties window

In the Recycle Bin Properties window there are several settings we can tweak. At the top of the window we can see the Recycle Bin Location. Recall that each drive has a Recycle Bin folder associated with it. From this list you can choose the Recycle Bin to work with. On the machine that figure 10.6 was taken from there is only one Recycle Bin but machines with several drives may have two or more.

Under "Settings for selected location" we can specify a maximum size. Remember the size specified is in megabytes, but the size shown under "Space Available" is in gigabytes. There are one thousand twenty four (1024) megabytes to a gigabyte, so the maximum size for this Recycle Bin is around the eight gigabyte mark. It is possible to increase or decrease that size by entering a new value in the Maximum size (MB): box, although for most users the default size is fine.

Below the Custom Size option is the option to disable the Recycle Bin altogether. If this option is chosen, the files are removed immediately when deleted. We do not recommend that beginners enable this option, in fact we don't recommend that anyone does. Having the safety net of the Recycle Bin is always a good idea.

Finally there is an option called "Display delete confirmation dialog". If you deselect this then Windows will not put up a window asking "Are you sure you want to remove this file?" when you delete a file. Again, we do not recommend deselecting this option.

When you are done configuring the Recycle Bin Properties, click on "Apply" and then "OK".

That concludes this lesson on the Recycle Bin and this chapter! You are now quite the competent Windows 7 user, give yourself a pat on the back for getting this far. The next chapter focuses on exploring other elements of Windows 7 and improving your skills further.

Chapter 4 – Polishing Your Skills

We have come so far and learned so much about Windows 7 since the start of this course. In this chapter we will be rounding off our tour of the various operating system elements.

Lesson 11 – Advanced Start Menu Options

In this lesson we are going to look at some of the advanced options for the Start Menu.

11.1 - Advanced options

To access the advanced Start Menu options, right click on the Start globe. This opens up a context menu, figure 11.1 shows the resulting menu:-

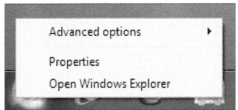

Figure 11.1 – The context menu from right clicking on the Start Globe. Note that the "Advanced options" sub-menu is part of our anti-virus package and may not appear on standard installations.

If you have used Windows before, you might be surprised to see that the context menu is significantly smaller than it was in either Windows Vista or Windows XP. Gone is the option to explore the Start Menu in Windows Explorer. If you liked to reorganise your Start Menu using this option, then sadly that is gone, although you can still do it with a little hidden folder browsing. We showed you how to view hidden folders in lesson 9.5.

Choosing "Properties" from the context menu will launch the Taskbar and Start Menu Properties window, figure 11.2 shows this window:-

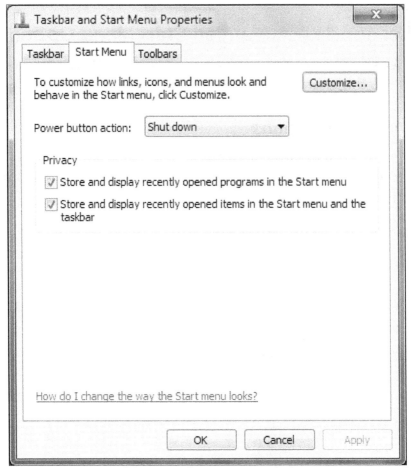

Figure 11.2 – Taskbar and Start Menu Properties window

In figure 11.2 we can see "Power Button action" near the top of the window. This refers to the physical power button on the front of a PC, or usually at the top of the keyboard on a laptop. You can change what happens when you press the button by using the drop down box. We covered what each of these options were way back in lesson 2.2.

Below the power button actions are the Privacy options. The first privacy option "Store and display recently opened programs in the Start menu" is fairly self explanatory. If you deselect this option then programs you launch will no longer show up on the recently used section of the Start Menu (this is the area at the top of the Start Menu below any items that are pinned).

The second option is "Store and display recently opened items in the Start menu and the taskbar". This option works with Windows 7's new Jump Lists feature. In lesson 2.1 we demonstrated how the "Getting started" item had it's own sub-menu. Certain items on the recently used section of a Windows 7 Start Menu will also have sub-menus. Figure 11.3 shows an example:-

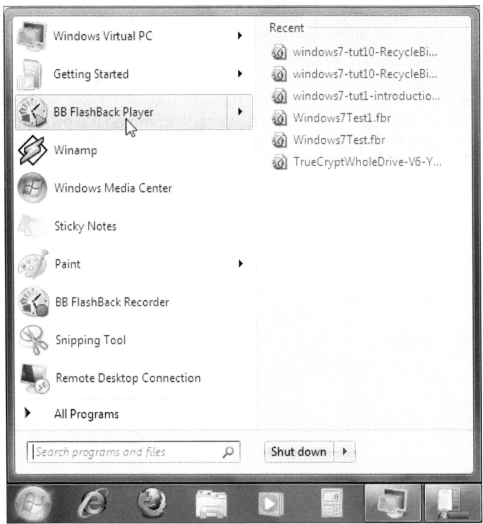

Figure 11.3 – Revealing the recently used "Jump List" for the program "BB Flashback Player"

In the example in figure 11.3, the user is hovering the mouse pointer over the "BB Flashback Player" icon (a third party program not included with Windows 7 as standard) and accessing the jump list of recently opened documents. If the BB Flashback player icon was pinned to the Taskbar, the same jump-list could be accessed by right clicking on the Taskbar icon.

If we were to deselect "Store and display recently opened items in the Start menu and the taskbar" in the Taskbar and Start Menu Properties window (figure 11.2) then recently opened documents will no longer appear in jump lists like this.

11.2 - Customize Start Menu

Refer back to figure 11.2, at the top of the window is a button labelled "Customize". Clicking on this button opens the window shown in figure 11.4:-

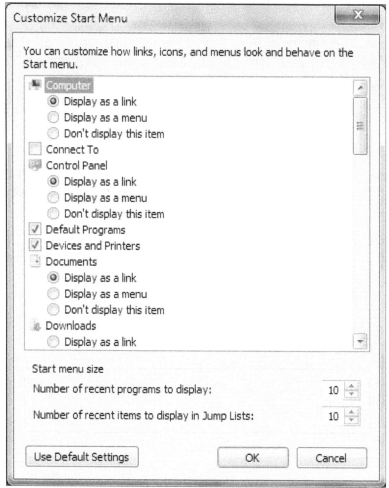

Figure 11.4 – Customizing the Start Menu

There are dozens of items we can add and customize on our Start Menu from this window. The items listed in the scroll box at the top of the window include various icons that we can add to the right of the Start Menu. There are so many different items that we cannot cover each individual one. Experiment on your own and remember that you can always click the "Use Default Settings" button at the bottom of the window to reset things back to the way they were.

Lots of the items have the option of displaying them as a link, as a menu or not at all. Items that are displayed as a link will appear simply as an icon on the Start Menu. Items that are displayed as a menu will have a sub-menu which you can open just like the jump lists we discussed previously.

In amongst the options to add new icons to your Start Menu there are some other options that affect the behaviour of your Start Menu. One potentially useful item is "Enable context menus and dragging and dropping". You will need to scroll down in order to find it. If you find that you are often accidentally reorganising your Start Menu because you mistakenly dragged an icon into another folder you might want to turn this option off. When this option is deselected, your icons are effectively locked in place on the Start Menu.

Also further down the list is "Open submenus when I pause on them with the mouse pointer". This option is enabled by default. If you deselect this option, then you will need to single click to open up sub-menus, rather than just hovering over them with the mouse pointer.

If you are a former Windows XP user you might be used to the "Run" command on your Start Menu. Using the Run command you can quickly launch a command such as "msconfig" to launch the System Configuration Utility. While the Run command is arguably redundant now that we can search for commands and programs from the Start Menu, you can still re-enable it. Scroll down in the list until you find "Run command" and then select it. If you never used Windows XP or don't really understand what a "Run" command would be used for then leave this option deselected.

The last option from this list that we will be discussing in detail is the "Use large icons" option. This option is right at the bottom of the list, it is enabled by default. Figure 11.5 shows an example of both small and large icons on a Start Menu:-

Figure 11.5 – Small icons (left) vs large icons (right) on a Start Menu

This option is entirely down to personal preference, small icons take up less space and therefore you can potentially show more icons on the Start Menu, large icons on the other hand are easier to recognise.

Below the long list of customization options in the Customize Start Menu window (figure 11.4) are two options under "Start menu size". The number of items to display in recent programs and in jump list menus can be changed. The maximum number of items is subject to space on your Start Menu, but feel free to experiment with any value you like. When you are done making customizations, don't forget to click "OK" to close the Customize Start Menu window and then "Apply" and "OK" to close the Taskbar and Start Menu Properties window.

That concludes our tour of Start Menu customization. We hope you enjoyed tweaking and personalising your Start Menu. In chapter 6 we will show you how you can personalise your copy of Windows 7 even further by changing your desktop backgrounds and other visual elements.

Lesson 12 – Computer

If you want to look at something on your computer, where better to go to than "Computer" ? From Computer (known as "My Computer" in Windows XP) you can get access or browse to all of the storage devices attached to your PC. You can open Computer by clicking on it from the Start Menu.

12.1 - Inside Computer

Figure 12.1 shows a typical "Computer" window:-

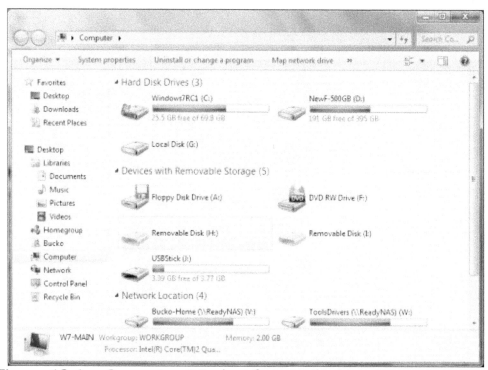

Figure 12.1 – Computer Window from a desktop PC with several drives

"Computer" will open in a familiar Windows Explorer window. The computer shown in figure 12.1 is a desktop computer with two hard drives, a DVD recorder drive, a floppy drive and several other removable drives, as well as several network drives.

12.2 - Hard disk drives

Every Windows 7 machine will have at least one hard drive. The machine in this example has two hard drives. (A third drive, Local Disk (G:) is actually an encrypted hard drive and not presently available for use). We can see at a glance how much space is free on each drive by looking at the blue bar or the values below (C: drive has 25.5 gigabytes (GB) free out of 69.8GB, for example). To get some more detailed information about a hard drive, right click on the drives icon and from the context menu choose "Properties". The drive Properties window will then open, figure 12.2 shows this window:-

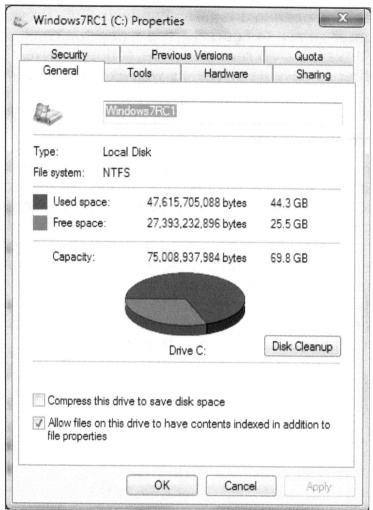

Figure 12.2 – General drive properties

We can see in figure 12.2 a pie chart which represents space on the drive. Free space in shown in purple and used space in blue. There are also two options below the pie chart:-

Compress this drive to save disk space:- When we talk about compressing data in computing it refers to the art of storing information more efficiently so that less space is consumed. By selecting this option to compress the drive, you might gain a little space on your hard drive but adversely it might degrade your computers performance. We recommend leaving this option disabled.

Allow files on this drive to have contents indexed in addition to file properties:- When this option is selected, Windows will add the contents of files such as word documents into the search index. Then, when you perform a search you can quickly search inside text files too. The only reasons to turn this option off are to improve disk performance on an older computer or to prevent sensitive file information being left in the search index.

12.3 - Devices with Removable Storage

Going back to Computer again, in figure 12.1 we can see a section called "Devices with Removable Storage". Floppy Disk Drive (A:) is an old fashioned floppy disk drive. Windows 7 still supports floppy disks; although they are obsolete by modern standards, many PC's still have floppy drives. Drives H: and I: are part of a memory card or storage card reader. Memory card readers accept storage cards that are commonly used in cameras, media players and even games consoles. Figure 12.3 shows a typical memory card reader:-

Figure 12.3 – A typical memory card reader

Drive F: is a DVD rewriter drive. Everyone should be familiar with CD's and DVD's, the universally popular format for storing music and videos. If your Windows 7 computer has a DVD rewriter drive, you can use it to play DVD videos (except on Windows 7 Starter and Home Basic editions) and also write your files to CD or DVD recordable discs.

Device J: is a portable USB stick drive or thumb drive. These are common portable storage devices that fit in your pocket and store gigabytes of information. They have virtually rendered the floppy disk obsolete.

Figure 12.4 – A Sandisk Cruzer USB stick drive. Actual length is around the length of an adult thumb, so these drives are often referred to as "thumb drives"

To browse any of the attached drives, simply double click on them. You might just be able to make out that drives H: and I: are slightly fainter, that is because there are currently no memory cards plugged into them. If you double click on an empty drive, Windows will prompt you with "Please insert a disk into Removable Disk". Disk in this context can refer to a storage card too.

12.4 - Network Location

The last section we can see in figure 12.1 is called "Network Location". If your computer is on a home or corporate network, you can create shortcuts to your most commonly used network locations by mapping a drive letter to them. To do this, choose "Map network drive" from the toolbar. You can then either enter the network address manually or browse across your network for the correct location.

12.5 - Other Devices

What other devices might we find in Computer? Some portable devices, such as media players, Personal Digital Assistants or Smartphones install their own special software. These devices then appear below Network Connections in their own category. Usually working with them is as easy as working with other storage devices, but consult the owners manual that came with the hardware for more details.

That concludes our tour of "Computer" in Windows 7. Now you understand how to access storage devices on your PC you will be ready for our tutorials on system backup which we cover in lesson 16.

Lesson 13 – More About The Taskbar

The Taskbar has seen some significant changes in Windows 7. Once you get used to the new features, they can actually be very helpful. In this lesson we will look at jump lists and Taskbar personalisation.

13.1 - Jump lists and the Taskbar

Many of the changes in Windows 7 are designed to help you work more quickly with your computer. Jump lists are one of the new features that appear throughout Windows 7. On the Taskbar they can be used to quickly jump to frequently used tasks in an application. To access the jump list for a program on the Taskbar, simply right click on the programs Taskbar icon, figure 13.1 shows Internet Explorers jump list:-

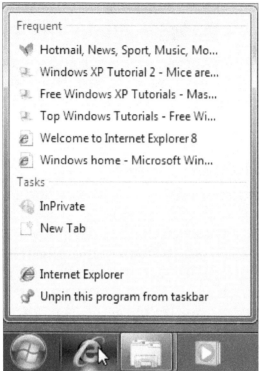

Figure 13.1 – Internet Explorer's jump list, accessed by right clicking on its icon

From Internet Explorer's jump list, we can go straight to one of our most frequently used websites. Under "Tasks" it is possible to switch to private surfing mode (InPrivate), that (supposedly at least) leaves behind no web history on the computer. We can also open a new tab or simply launch internet explorer as normal by choosing "Internet Explorer". We take a brief tour of Internet Explorer 8 in lesson 34.

Notice that Internet Explorer does not have to be running in order to access its jump list.

Any program pinned to the Taskbar can have its own jump list. Usually for older (pre Windows 7) software the jump list simply includes the most recently opened documents or the most frequently opened files or folders. Programs that are Windows

7 aware can have their own custom jump lists. Figure 13.2 shows the jump list from Windows Media Player:-

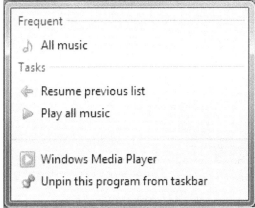

Figure 13.2 – Jump list from Windows Media Player

Just like the Internet Explorer 8 jump list, Windows Media Player lists the most frequently used media or play lists at the top and then additional tasks below them.

13.2 - Moving the Taskbar

There are several customizations we can do with the Taskbar. The most simple being moving and resizing it. Before you can move the Taskbar, it needs to be unlocked. Right click on the Taskbar and deselect the "Lock the Taskbar" option, as shown in figure 13.3:-

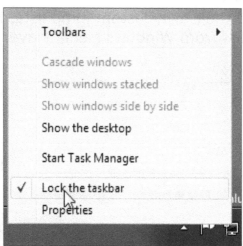

Figure 13.3 – Before the Taskbar can be moved or resized it must be unlocked

When the Taskbar is unlocked it can be moved to any screen edge. This is done by clicking and holding down the mouse button and then dragging the mouse towards one of the screen edges. The Taskbar can also be resized in the same way we resized a window in lesson 3.2 by moving the mouse to the edge of the Taskbar and dragging it upwards. A bigger Taskbar is often useful on powerful machines with large monitors. When there are lots of programs open at once, a bigger Taskbar gets less cluttered.

It is a good idea to lock the Taskbar again when you are done moving and/or resizing it. If you do not, you are likely to accidentally move or size it as you work with your PC.

13.3 - Adding Toolbars to the Taskbar

There are several optional toolbars that can be added to the Taskbar. To add a toolbar, right click on the Taskbar and choose "Toolbars". Figure 13.4 shows the available toolbars:-

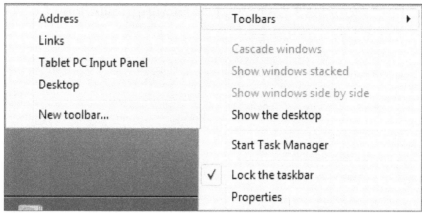

Figure 13.4 – Choosing a toolbar to add to the Taskbar

Let's see what each of these toolbars does.

Address:- Enables the user to enter a web address or local address or path directly into the Taskbar.

Links:- This toolbar enables you to quickly jump to your favourite internet links which you added to your "favorites" in Internet Explorer (see lesson 35.3)

Tablet PC Input Panel:- If you are lucky enough to have a touchscreen or stylus operated computer then the Tablet PC Input Panel provides a handy toolbar to make working without a keyboard much easier.

Desktop:- Provides links to common locations on the computer and on the desktop.

New toolbar:- Creates a custom toolbar. Choosing "New Toolbar..." opens up a file browser window. Simply browse to any folder on your PC and choose "Select Folder". The content from that folder will then be available from the Taskbar.

13.4 - Other Taskbar Customizations

There are several other customization options for the Taskbar. To access them, right click on the Taskbar and choose

"Properties".Figure 13.5 shows the resulting window:-

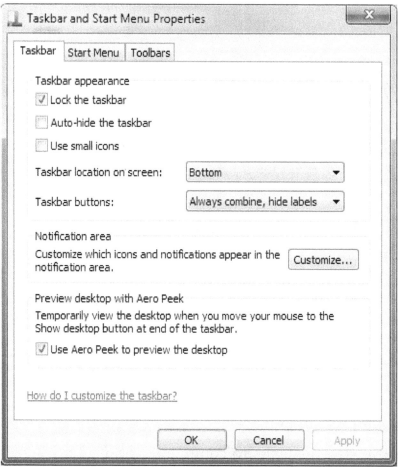

Figure 13.5 – Taskbar and Start Menu Properties Window

Under "Taskbar appearance" there are several options. We already covered the "Lock the taskbar" option. "Auto-hide the taskbar" makes the Taskbar automatically shrink down out of sight when it is not used. To reveal it again, move the mouse pointer to the bottom of the screen (or the edge of the screen where the Taskbar is positioned), the Taskbar will then reappear. This option is useful on smaller monitors where screen space is at a premium.

Selecting "Use small icons" reduces the size of program icons on your Taskbar, figure 13.6 shows an example of this:-

Figure 13.6 – Small icons Vs large icons on a Windows 7 Taskbar

Using the "Taskbar location on screen:" menu, it is possible to reposition the Taskbar automatically, rather than by dragging it.

Below this control is the "Taskbar buttons:" control, figure 13.7 shows the available options:-

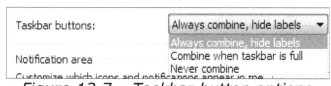

Figure 13.7 – Taskbar button options

Each option will change how the icons are displayed on your Taskbar. We will take a detailed look at each option below:-

Always combine, hide labels:- This is the default setting you have been using while working through this course. Icons will appear on your Taskbar without labels. Windows from the same applications will stack on top of each other.

Combine when taskbar is full:- This makes the Taskbar behave more like it did in previous versions of Windows. Icons for programs will be displayed next to a label indicating the window title. Figure 13.8 shows an example of this:-

Figure 13.8 – A Taskbar set to "Combine when taskbar is full" mode

Never combine:- Works the same as "Combine when taskbar is full", except that as the Taskbar fills up, Windows won't combine related windows (e.g multiple Windows Explorer windows) into groups.

Finally, it is possible to disable the Aero Peek button (the button at the end of the Taskbar that we showed you way back in lesson 1) by deselecting the "Use Aero Peek to preview the desktop" option.

When you are done making changes, be sure to click on "Apply" to make them take effect.

That concludes our tour of Taskbar customization. In the next lesson we will take a more detailed look at another component that has changed significantly in Windows 7, the notification area or system tray as it is sometimes called.

Lesson 14 – The Notification Area

The notification area is another part of Windows 7 that has been significantly overhauled. The notification area is often called the system tray, though the official Microsoft name has always been "notification area". It was introduced as a place for programs which generally ran in the background and did not need a window permanently open. Software such as antivirus packages or automatic backup tools can place small notification icons in this area. From these icons users can see at a glance that the program is running normally, or the program can notify the user that it needs their attention.

14.1 - The new notification area versus the old

As computers became faster and equipped with more memory and other resources, many users started installing all kinds of programs that utilised the notification area. As a result, it became very cluttered. It is not uncommon for systems to have more than twenty of these little icons and it quickly becomes unmanageable.

Figure 14.1 – A cluttered notification area from a Windows XP machine

Windows 7 tackles this problem by redesigning the notification area. The most important or frequently used icons can still be present on the Taskbar, while the rest are hidden away in a pop-up menu and only appear if they need your attention. Figure 14.2 shows the Windows 7 notification area:-

Figure 14.2 – A Windows 7 notification area

In the picture we can see three notification icons that are permanently displayed. The flag shaped icon is the Action Center. This notifies you about potential problems on your PC, such as security alerts. Next to that is the network icon, this can be used for connecting quickly to networks, both wired and wireless. Then there is the volume icon, a quick click of this accesses a sliding control which can adjust the volume level for all sounds on your computer.

In figure 14.2 we can also see that by clicking the arrow icon, we get a pop up menu showing us another notification icon. This is an antivirus package. If the antivirus needs to notify us of something the message will still appear in the notification area, but otherwise the icon is hidden away. To access additional settings for the antivirus package or any application running in the notification area, simply open the pop-up menu and then click on the programs icon.

14.2 - Customizing the notification area

If you have an application that you access regularly from the notification area, you may want to make it appear permanently like the three default icons. To do this, first open the pop up menu (as shown in figure 14.2) then choose "Customize...". Figure 14.3 shows the window which will then appear:-

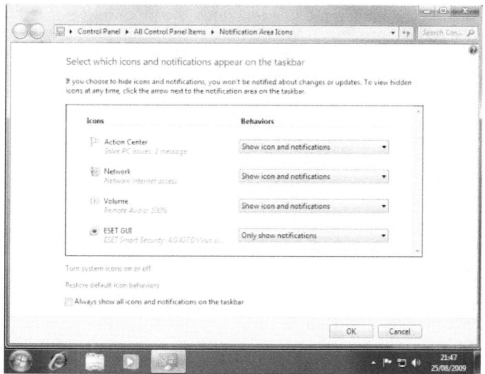

Figure 14.3 – Customization options for the notification area

The list in the window above shows all the items in the notification area, including the default Windows 7 ones. From this list we can change the behaviour of each icon/program. Notice how ESET GUI is set to "Only show notifications". With this setting, the program icon will be hidden unless it needs to notify the user of anything.

The three default notification icons, Action Center, Network and Volume have their behaviours set to "Show icon and notifications". With this setting they will always appear in the notification area.

There is one other setting that we can choose, that is "Hide icon and notifications" With this setting, the icon will still appear in the pop up menu (figure 14.2), however Windows will suppress any notification messages the program sends and the icon will remain in the hidden menu even when the program wants to notify you of something. We do not recommend using this setting with software such as antivirus packages that may need to inform you of possible security problems.

Finally, right at the bottom of the window is the option to "Always show all icons and notifications on the taskbar". This reverts back to the classic behaviour described at the start of the lesson. If you don't have many notification area icons you might prefer to do this, but for most of us the new way is a big improvement.

That concludes this lesson on the Windows 7 notification area. Don't forget that although the notification area icons are hidden away more neatly in Windows 7, they still represent programs that are running and therefore consuming computer resources. If you let too many of these programs run, you will start to slow your computer down, so be careful not to install too many. In the next lesson we will look at Windows 7's extensive in-built search options.

Lesson 15 – Search Is Everywhere

In Windows 7, as was the case with Windows Vista, search is built into almost everything. In lesson 2.3 we showed you how to search from the Start Menu. It is also possible to search from Windows Explorer windows and in places such as the Control Panel. Windows 7 search is a powerful tool and learning how to use it correctly can make you super productive.

15.1 - Tags and other meta data

Meta data (data about data) enables you to add descriptive information to files to help you find them more quickly. Just like you might add coloured stickers to items you file in a filing cabinet, in Windows 7 you can add tags to your data. Figure 15.1 shows the available meta data for a picture file:-

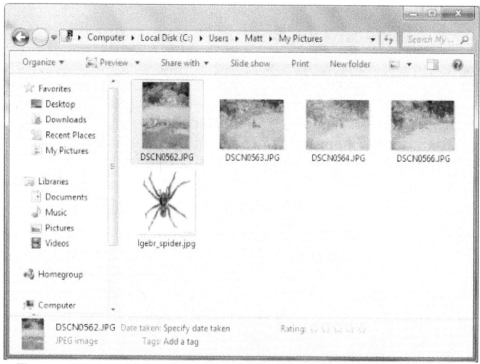

*Figure 15.1 – Meta data for DSCN0562 can be seen at the
bottom of the Windows Explorer window*

The meta data for the image is shown at the bottom of the
window. We can specify the date taken, a rating out of five and
add a tag. Tags are probably the most useful types of meta data
to add to pictures. To add a tag, click on "Add a tag" and type a
descriptive tag for this image, for example "garden", since this
is a scene from a garden. Press the Enter key to save a tag or
press the right arrow key and enter another tag. You can add as
many tags as you like by doing this, just press Enter when you
are finished.

Once you have tagged an image, you can search for it from the
Start Menu, just like we did in lesson 2.3. Any images tagged
"garden" for example, would show up in a Start Menu search for
"garden". If you tag all your pictures with descriptive tags, you
will be able to locate them much more quickly.

15.2 - Indexing options

Windows can find information on your PC more quickly by using a search index. Files that are indexed have a reference to them in a giant search index or catalogue that Windows 7 maintains. In this lesson we will take a look at the indexing options. You can access these options from the Control Panel or more simply by searching for "indexing options" from the Start Menu and then clicking the icon that appears. Figure 15.2 shows the Indexing Options window:-

Figure 15.2 – Indexing Options

In figure 15.2 we can see the default indexing options. Under

"Included Locations" you can see which places on your computer are added to the index. By clicking "Modify" it is possible to add other locations to the index, although we can only add locations on local drives, not network drives.

Click on the "Advanced" button to change the advanced options. Figure 15.3 shows the advanced indexing options:-

Figure 15.3 – Advanced indexing options

Under "File Settings" we can firstly choose to index encrypted files. This only applies to Windows encrypted files and not, for example, Truecrypt or PGP encrypted files. This option is off by default as it represents a security risk, since the contents of the encrypted file can be stored in the index in an unencrypted state. This option might not be present on all versions of Windows 7 and we do not cover encrypted files or Bitlocker in this course.

The second option under File Settings is "Treat similar words with diacritics as different words". What are diacritics? Diacritics are often called accents (though in actual fact an accent is only one of many different types of diacritic), and the English language doesn't generally use them. In other languages, such as French, they can be applied to letters to change the pronunciation. For example 'é' and 'e' are distinct because of the diacritic on the first letter.

If you regularly work with other languages you may wish to turn this option on, but for those of us who work only in English, it can safely stay off.

Under "Troubleshooting" is the option to rebuild the index. If you find yourself searching for files and getting no results back, there is the possibility that the index is corrupt. Click on "Rebuild" to rebuild and repair it. Normally you will not need to do this as Windows is capable of maintaining the index on its own.

Finally, under "Index Location", it is possible to move the index to another drive. If you have a secondary hard drive it may be faster to store the search index separately from the Windows system drive, though for most users the default location is fine.

Clicking on the "File types" tab at the top of the window lists the current file types that are indexed. Figure 15.4 shows this window:-

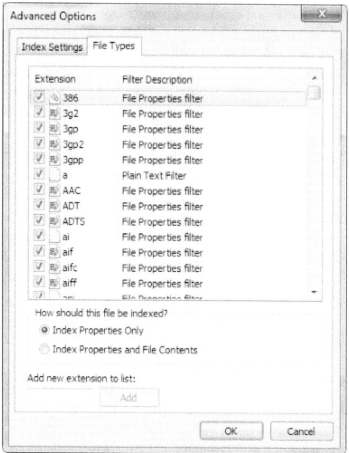

Figure 15.4 – Windows indexes hundreds of different file types

You can see from figure 15.4 that Windows knows about and indexes all kinds of files. For some types of file such as plain text or Microsoft Word documents, Windows will also index the contents of these documents.

At the bottom of the window you can add your own file types just by typing in the file extension (we covered file extensions in lesson 9.6). If the file does not contain text, you should choose "Index Properties Only" to avoid cluttering up the index with junk data, since Windows isn't clever enough to recognise file contents in picture or sound files just yet.

When you are done changing indexing options, click on "OK".

15.3 - Tips for searching in Windows 7

Not being able to find what you are looking for is frustrating and the nice thing about storing information digitally is that computers can look for things much quicker than we can in the physical world. Having said that, computers are pretty dumb, so be sure to tell yours exactly what you are looking for and where, to avoid frustration. Here are a couple of tips to help with the searching process.

When searching in Windows Explorer, the search starts from the current location:- If you use the built in search in Windows Explorer, keep in mind that it does not search your entire computer. For example, if you are in your video folder and you search for a photograph, it is unlikely that the search will find anything (unless you are in the habit of storing photographs in your video folder). The search will only search within the current folder and any sub-folders in that folder.

Searching in Windows Explorer does not search through tags or meta data:- If you want to find a picture you tagged, search from the Start Menu not from Windows Explorer.

Use search filters to filter results:- If you are searching for a photograph, video or music file, let Windows know that you are not interested in text files or other types of file by telling it exactly what type of file you want to find. Click on the search box to choose a filter or modifier, figure 15.5 shows an example of this:-

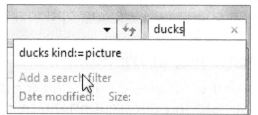

Figure 15.5 – Adding a search filter

Be sure to try these techniques for yourself. The Windows 7 search facilities are powerful. Learn to use them and you will potentially save yourself a lot of time.

That is the end of this lesson and this chapter. The next chapter deals with computer and data security, starting with lesson 16 which deals with backing up your computer, a very important subject that many users still neglect.

Chapter 5 – Securing Your PC And Your Data

If you have been following this course so far, you are probably excited to dive head-first into your new Windows 7 PC and start changing, tweaking and trying all kinds of things. Indeed, we encourage you to do this, it is the best way to learn. Before you start getting too carried away however, it is time to consider security, the security of your computer and your important data.

This chapter firstly tackles the subject of backup. An alarming number of people still do not backup their data at all. Computer hard drives are mechanical devices and will eventually fail through wear and tear. Without a proper backup strategy, any information you have on a hard drive which fails may well be lost forever.

Once we are done backing our system up, we will look at the various security mechanisms in Windows itself. We will show you how to create additional accounts for other family members and how to secure your account against malicious software, using User Account Controls. If you plan to go online with your computer you should understand about security software including Antivirus software, the Windows 7 firewall and about keeping your PC up-to-date.

Lesson 16 – Planning A Backup Strategy

It is important to remember that files and folders on your PC can vanish into oblivion at any time if you do not have a proper backup strategy. Hard drive failures are the most common hardware fault on modern PC's. While it is more usual for a hard drive to fail when it is old, it is not uncommon for hard drives to fail randomly at any time.

In this lesson we will discuss how to plan a backup strategy around the capabilities of the Windows 7 backup utility. If you are planning to use a third party backup solution this lesson might also be useful to you, but it is focused on the backup utility provided with Windows 7.

16.1 - Backup methodologies

Using the new Windows 7 backup software is not too complicated but understanding what to backup often is. Luckily Windows 7 backup supports two different kinds of backup, image backup and scheduled backup. What is the difference between these two options?

Image backup:- This option takes a snapshot of your entire computer, you can think of it like creating a time capsule and putting your current hard drive inside it. When you restore from an image backup, all data on your hard drive reverts to the state it was in when the backup was taken. You cannot restore individual files from an image backup (this is true in Windows 7 backup, though some third party backup solutions do not have this restriction). You can however, restore your computer in the event of a total failure of your computers hard drive or operating system.

Scheduled backup:- This option backs up individual files and folders. It can backup several versions of a file and restore the backups at any time. This type of backup is often called a file backup or file level backup in third party backup utilities. A

scheduled backup cannot backup critical operating system files
however and cannot be used to recover from a hard drive
failure without first restoring from an image backup.

Consider the information on your computer, we can split it
roughly into two categories:-

Programs - These are the things you install and run on your
computer, including the actual operating system itself. It also
includes word processors, web browsers, games, music players
and anything and everything that runs on your computer. It
changes infrequently compared with data.

Data - This is information that programs work with. It includes
word processor documents, spreadsheets, music and video files,
digital photographs, saved game positions and anything and
everything that the programs you run on your computer work
with.

Data is personal to you and usually needs extra protection
compared with programs which can usually be reinstalled from
their original media or from the internet. Making regular
scheduled backups of your data and occasional image backups
is the ideal way to protect your operating system and luckily
this is what Windows 7 backup will do. For novice users, this
takes away the headache of considering backup strategies on
your own.

16.2 - Do you have an operating system recovery disc?

There may come a time when you want to revert your computer
back to the state it was in when you first bought it. Perhaps you
have clogged your computer up with too much third party
software and you just want a clean start, or maybe you are
selling your PC and want to make sure that no unlicensed
software or personal information remains on it. Either way, you
will need an operating system recovery DVD.

If you purchased your copy of Windows 7 from a store, your
operating system recovery DVD is the same DVD you used to

install Windows 7 in the first place, so you are covered. If you purchased your computer with Windows 7 pre installed, the manufacturer might not have provided an operating system recovery disc. Some manufacturers include a special recovery file/partition on the computers hard drive instead of a DVD. This is fine unless your hard drive fails (and your hard drive will eventually fail). If you do not have a recovery DVD or some way of resetting your PC back to factory fresh, you should make one now. We will show you how in lesson 20.

16.3 - Where to backup

If you are still reeling from the cost of buying your new PC, you won't be happy to discover that you are going to need to spend a little more money on a backup solution. However, backing up to the same hard drive is just not an option. If your hard drive fails then so does your backup. The Windows 7 backup utility gives you three options for backup media, external drives, DVD recordable and network drives. Let's take a look at each option now:-

External drives:- External drives usually connect by USB, though some connect via other kinds of interface such as eSATA and (increasingly rarely) Firewire. External drives provide easily expandable storage that is ideal for backup. Most, if not all modern Windows computers have USB connectors. Figure 16.1 shows two USB ports:-

Figure 16.1 – Two USB ports on a computer, notice the white USB "octopus" logo at the top left

When choosing an external drive, choose one that is bigger than the system drive in your PC. At least twice as much capacity is desirable, so there is plenty of room for your backups. Remember that we showed you how to determine the capacity of a hard drive in lesson 12.2. Figure 16.2 shows a typical external hard drive that connects to the computer via USB.

Figure 16.2 – A typical external hard drive. Like the vast majority of external drives, this drive connects via USB

Let's look at the advantages and disadvantages of external hard drives for backup now.

Advantages:- Fast, affordable high capacity storage. Hard drives continue to increase in capacity and decrease in price.

Disadvantages:- User must remember to connect the hard drive prior to the scheduled backup.

DVD recordable (DVD-R) or re-recordable (DVD-RW) discs:- Once the backup and archival medium of choice for home users, DVD-R discs are rapidly being replaced by hard drives which continue to tumble in price. DVD recordable discs store a maximum of around 4 gigabytes (single layer) or just under 8 gigabytes (dual layer). Only certain types of drive can record on dual layer discs and you should check your computers documentation before buying these types of disc. The capacity of DVD's once seemed huge but now seems paltry. Figure 16.3 shows a typical consumer pack of DVD recordable discs:-

Figure 16.3 – pack of 50 DVD-R discs suitable for backup. This pack provides around 215 gigabytes of storage, modest by modern standards

Let's look at the advantages and disadvantages of DVD-R discs now.

Advantages:- Your PC may already be equipped with a DVD recorder and if so, DVD recordable discs are a very low cost backup option.

Disadvantages:- Slow to record, limited capacities, highest capacity dual layer discs cannot be re-written, requires user intervention to swap discs during a backup.

Local network backup:- This is only an option for those using either third party backup software or Windows 7 Professional, Enterprise and Ultimate editions.

Once the exclusive realm of businesses, network backup around the home is gaining in popularity. Using network storage can be more convenient than attaching an external hard drive. As long as the network is available any and all computers in your home can access network attached storage. It is usually much easier to remember to leave your laptops Wi-Fi network enabled while you work rather than having to lug in an external drive and attach it. Figure 16.4 shows a network attached storage device (NAS):-

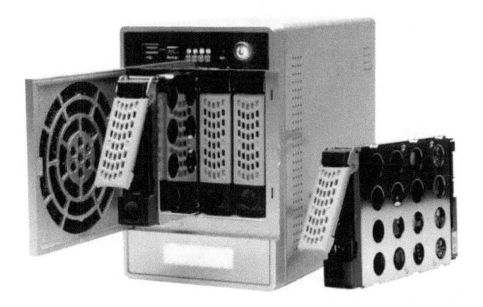

Figure 16.4 – More expensive network storage solutions like this Netgear ReadyNAS can hold multiple hard drives which copy or mirror each other, providing some protection against random hard drive failure

Network backup solutions can be expensive however and they

often require technical configuration to get the best out of them. If you are unable to start your operating system and you need to recover from an image backup, you may find that your computer cannot connect to the network and thus your backup is inaccessible.

Let's sum up the advantages and disadvantages of network backup now:-

Advantages:- Convenient, can be used by several computers in the house. Backups are fast and can be configured to work automatically with little or no user intervention.

Disadvantages:- Relatively expensive, may require expert configuration, restoring image backups from the network is usually not possible. **Windows 7 Home and Starter editions do not support network backup at all**.

In this guide, we will be showing you how to backup using an external USB hard drive, as that is the configuration that we recommend for home users. We will also show you how to create a rescue DVD so that you can restore from your backup in the event of a hard drive or operating system failure.

16.4 - A note about storing your backups

Remember that hard drive failure and system crashes are not the only disaster you may encounter. Fire, theft, natural disaster and other unfortunate accidents could see both your computer and your backup copy wiped out in one go. To mitigate this danger, you might want to store backup copies at a friends house (you could store his or her backups in exchange) or perhaps in a locked drawer at the office. Another option is to use one of the many new online backup services which backup your data and save it in several data centres. We don't cover online backup in this guide since the Windows 7 backup utility does not directly support it, but you may wish to investigate this option particularly if you run your business from home.

That concludes this lesson on preparing your backup strategy.

Once you have purchased your external hard drive or backup solution of choice, we can enable automatic backup in Windows 7 easily, we will show you how in the next lesson.

Lesson 17 – Configuring Automatic Backup

As mentioned in the previous lesson, the Windows 7 backup utility is vastly improved when compared with the Windows Vista version. In this lesson we will configure the backup utility to protect the computer.

17.1 - Setting up a backup

The first thing to do is launch the backup utility. It is available through the Control Panel under "System and Security". It can also be launched from the Start Menu by searching for "backup and restore" and then clicking the icon that appears. Figure 17.1 below shows the Backup and Restore window:-

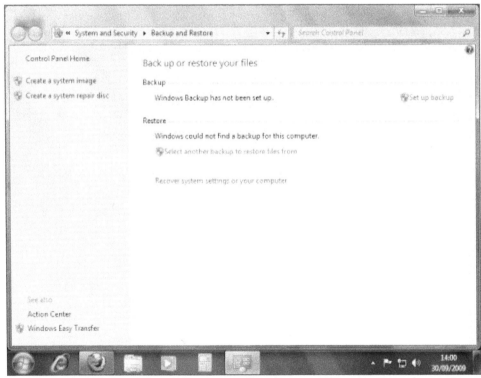

Figure 17.1 – The Windows Backup utility in Windows 7

The first order of business is to set up a backup. Attach your external hard drive if you are using one, and then click on "Set up backup" near the top right of the window. The window shown in figure 17.2 will then appear:-

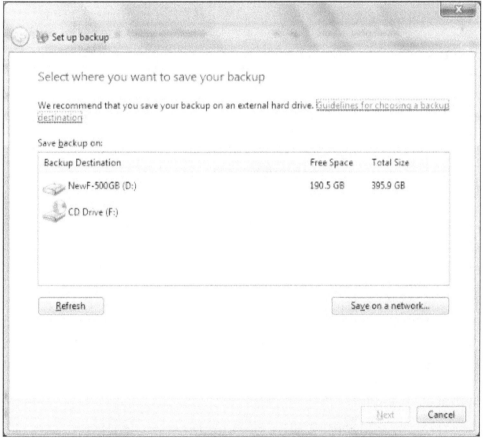

Figure 17.2 – Choosing a backup location

Choose a backup destination. We covered different backup destinations in the previous lesson, but this step trips up a lot of users so be sure to pay attention to the on screen prompts. You should also review the previous lesson if necessary and optionally click on the "Guidelines for choosing a backup destination" link (see figure 17.2) to learn more. This guide will focus on using a secondary hard drive (usually an external hard drive) for storing backups.

Choose a backup location by clicking on it. If the backup utility suspects that the location you choose is not suitable it will warn you, see figure 17.3 for an example:-

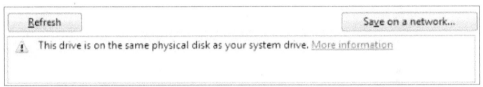

Figure 17.3 – Pay attention to what the Backup Utility tells you down at the bottom of the window when choosing a backup location

In this case, the backup utility knows this is not a good place to store a backup because this is the same physical hard drive. Hard drives can be split or partitioned into two or more separate sections which appear in Windows as distinct drives but are physically still on the same hard disk. It is unlikely that your system will be configured like this, since doing so requires special software and a smattering of technical know how. Even so, this serves as a good example of how the backup utility can help you choose a suitable backup location if you pay attention to what it is saying.

When you have decided on a backup location, click on "Next". You will then see the window shown in figure 17.4.

17.2 - Choosing what to backup

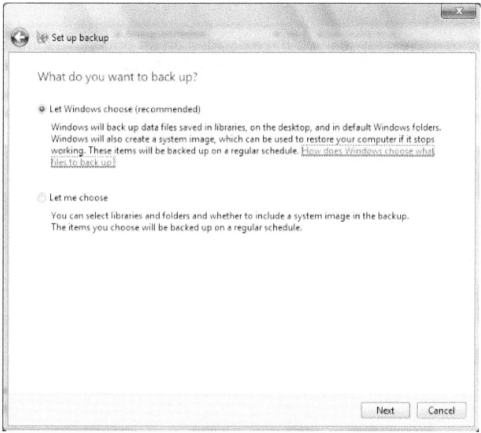

Figure 17.4 – Choosing a backup option

In figure 17.4, the backup utility asks if we want to let Windows choose which files to backup, or if we prefer to select them ourselves.

We recommend that you let Windows choose. If you do, all data in your personal folders and libraries will be backed up. The backup also includes a system image which can be used to restore the PC in the event of a complete failure of the computers hard drive or operating system.

If you opt to choose files manually, you will be presented with a file browser to choose which files to include. We don't cover this in this lesson, but if you have completed the lessons on Windows Explorer you should have no difficulty navigating to your files.

Click on "Next" when you have decided on an option. Assuming you opted to let Windows choose what files to backup, you will see the window shown in figure 17.5:-

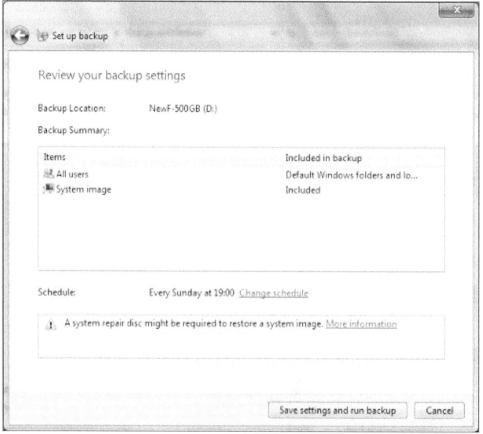

Figure 17.5 – Review your backup settings

The backup is now ready to go. You can check your settings one last time, then click on "Save settings and run backup". By default Windows sets up the backup to run "Every Sunday at 19:00" (7pm). If this isn't convenient, you can click on "Change schedule" and use the window that then appears to select a different day. You can even change the backup to run monthly or daily if you prefer.

When you are done checking settings and changing schedules, click on "Save settings and run backup". You will then be returned to the Backup and Restore window and a backup will start immediately. When it has finished, your backup and restore window should look like figure 17.6:-

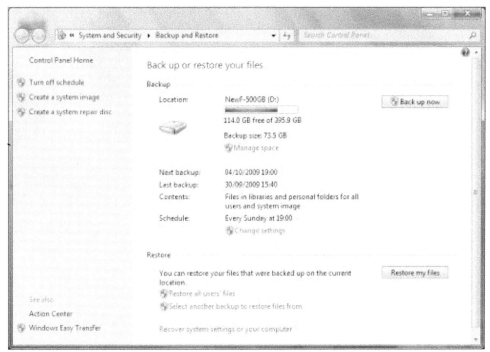

Figure 17.6 – Backup and Restore window following a successful backup

You can now close the Backup and Restore window and go back to working with your PC. Your backups will take place at their scheduled time, don't forget to attach your external drive if necessary.

17.3 - System Repair Disc

Windows 7 lets us create a system repair disc. We can use this in place of an operating system recovery DVD, if your computer manufacturer did not include one. If you do not already have one we strongly suggest creating one. We cover how to make a system repair disc in lesson 20.

That concludes this lesson. In the next lesson we will demonstrate how to get files from out of a backup and back onto your PC.

Lesson 18 – Restoring Files From A Backup

Backup copies are useless if you cannot easily restore data from them. In this lesson we will show you how to restore your data from a scheduled (file level) backup.

18.1 - Restoring files

To begin restoring files from a backup, make sure your backup drive/device is connected and then open the Backup and Restore section of the Control Panel (just like we did in lesson 17.1). The window should appear and look like the one shown in figure 17.6. Click on the button labelled "Restore my files" to start the restoration process. Figure 18.1 shows the window which will now appear:-

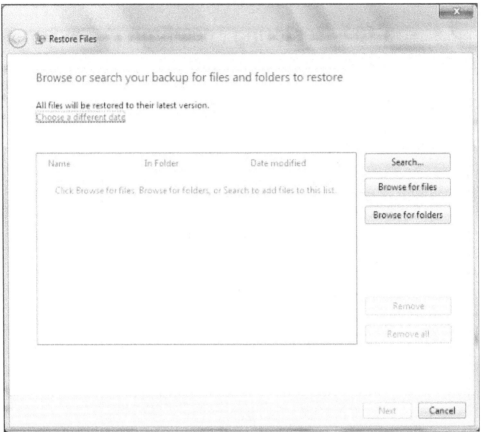

Figure 18.1 – Choosing files to restore from a backup

When you restore files from a backup, then by default the files will be restored from the most recent backup. To restore from an earlier backup, choose "Choose a different date" from the top of the window. You will then be able to browse through older backup sets.

To restore a file, click on "Browse for files". To restore a whole folder, click on "Browse for folders". You can restore any combination of files and folders. When you choose either "Browse for files" or "Browse for folders", you will see a familiar file browser window appear. Use this to navigate to the file or folder you want to restore. Figure 18.2 shows a Restore Files window with one file and one folder selected for recovery:-

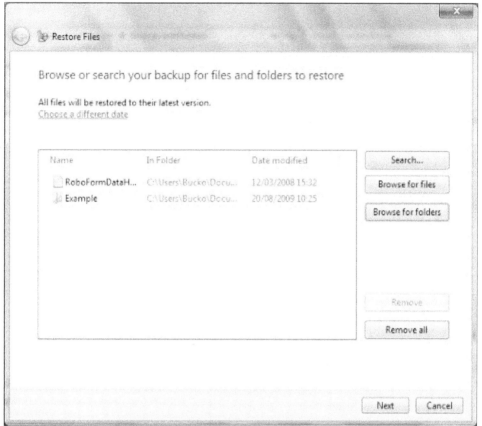

Figure 18.2 – Ready to restore one file and one folder. You can add as many files and folders to this list as you like

When you are finished choosing files and folders to restore, click on "Next". The window shown in figure 18.3 will then appear:-

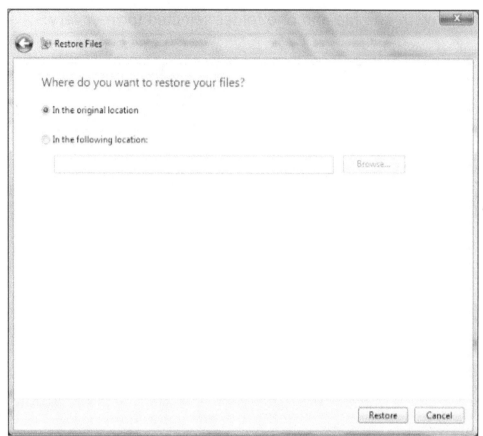

Figure 18.3 – Choosing where to restore the files

18.2 - Choosing a location for restored files

In figure 18.3, the backup utility asks us where to restore the files to. You can opt to restore the files to their original location or you can restore to a different location. If you restore to the original location and there are still copies of those files in this location, they will be overwritten by the files in the backup. Care must be taken therefore not to overwrite a more recent copy with one from your backup. If in doubt, restore to a different location by choosing "In the following location:" and then clicking "Browse..." to locate a temporary folder.

When you are ready to restore your files, click on "Restore". The restoration process will take anywhere from a couple of seconds to several hours, depending on the size and quantity of the files you are restoring. When the process is complete, you will be given the option of viewing your restored files. Click on the link and Windows Explorer will open, allowing you to browse the files.

That concludes this lesson on restoring files from a scheduled or file level backup. In the next lesson, we will look at restoring from a system image.

Lesson 19 – Restoring Your Computer From A System Image

To protect against system failure and hard drive failure, Windows 7 also includes image backup facilities. Image backups are like snapshots of your computer and can restore your entire operating system back to the way it was months or even years ago.

19.1 - Restoring a system image

In this lesson we will take you through the steps involved in restoring a system image from within Windows. To get started, firstly connect your backup drive if you have not done so already, then open the Backup and Restore section of the Control Panel just like we did in lesson 17.1. This time, click on "Recover system settings or your computer". This option is at the very bottom of the window. You will then see the window shown in figure 19.1:-

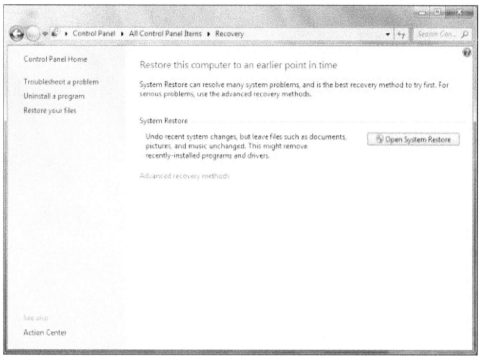

Figure 19.1 – System restore maybe a quicker option than restoring a system image

If you are restoring a system image because Windows has malfunctioned, then normally you would try the system restore function first. We cover system restore in lesson 44. If that fails or if you want to restore a system image for any reason, click on "Advanced recovery methods". The window shown in figure 19.2 will then appear:-

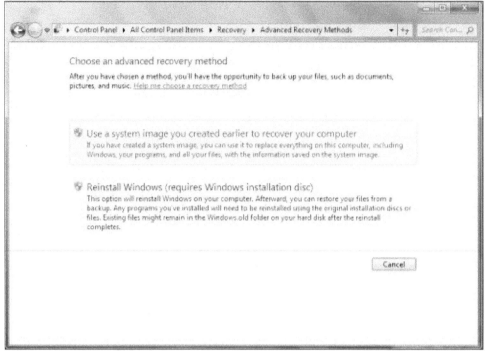

Figure 19.2 – Recovering or reinstalling the operating system through the advanced recovery methods

In this lesson we are going to restore from a system image, so choose "Use a system image you created earlier to recover your computer". The window shown in figure 19.3 will then appear:-

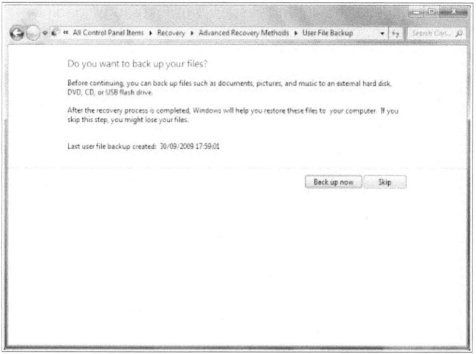

Figure 19.3 – Any files not backed up before restoring a system image will be lost or replaced with earlier versions

The backup utility now gives us the option of backing up our files. Remember that when you restore a system image, every single file and folder on your computer is restored back to the way it was when the system image was taken. It is just as if we are rewinding our computer to the time when we took the image. That means, any files or folders we have changed or added since then will be lost, unless we back them up.

If you decide to backup now (and we strongly recommend you do) then click on "Back up now". You will then create a scheduled or file level backup just like we did in lesson 17.

19.2 - Recovery mode

Once the backup is complete (or skipped) the backup utility will prompt you to restart your computer. Click on "Restart" and

Windows will shut down and restart, but instead of loading
Windows again, the system will reboot into recovery mode,
figure 19.4 shows you what to expect:-

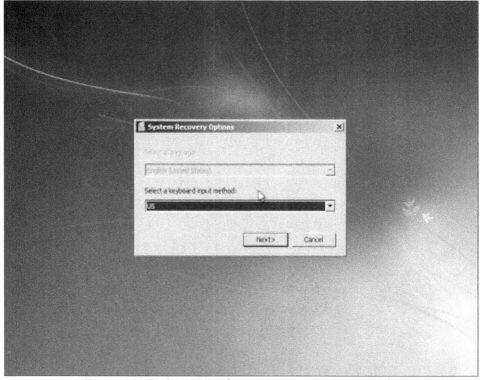

Figure 19.4 – Windows in recovery mode

To start the recovery process, choose your preferred keyboard
layout and then click on "Next >". You should then see the
window shown in figure 19.5:-

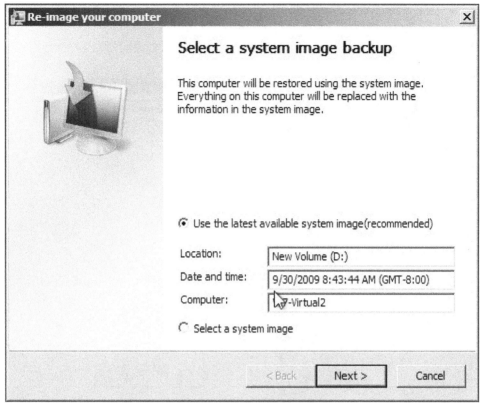

Figure 19.5 – Windows should automatically detect the latest system image

As long as you attached your backup hard drive before starting this process, Windows should detect the latest system image automatically. If you want to restore from a different image, choose "Select a system image". You will then be able to browse for the correct image. In this example we are going to use the latest image and simply click on "Next >". A window with some advanced restore options will then appear. These options are for advanced users and we don't cover them in this guide, so simply click on "Next >" again. The window shown in figure 19.6 will then appear:-

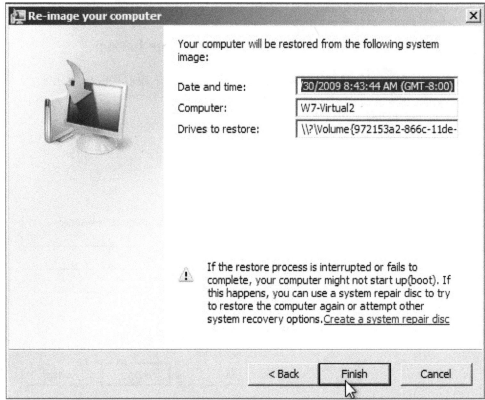

Figure 19.6 – Re-imaging is ready to begin

The restore process is now ready to begin, make sure that nobody cuts the power to the computer during the restoration process. If you are using a notebook/laptop style computer, make sure it is plugged in and preferably fully charged. If the power is cut off to your computer you may need to use a system repair disc to restart the process from the beginning.

When you are ready to proceed, click on "Finish". Windows will warn you one last time that all data on your hard drive will be overwritten with the data in the system image. Click on "Yes". The window shown in figure 19.7 will then appear:-

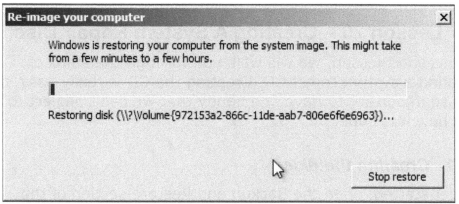

Figure 19.7 – Re-imaging (restoring from a system image) in progress

The window tells us that the process might take "from a few minutes to a few hours". Usually, the time taken is considerably nearer the few hours end of that scale. When the restoration is complete, Windows will reboot automatically. Your system is now restored from the image backup, you can now open the Backup and Restore Control Panel item and restore any new files you backed up before the process started.

That concludes this lesson on restoring system image backups. In the next lesson we will show you how to create a rescue disc and then you can consider yourself fully backup savvy!

Lesson 20 – Creating A System Repair Disc

In this short lesson, we will walk you through the steps of creating a system repair CD. Creating the CD is really easy, but it is so important to have one handy that we can't neglect to tell you how it is done.

20.1 - Creating the disc

To get started, open the Backup and Restore section of the Control Panel just like we did in lesson 17. Now, from the options on the left of the window, choose "Create a system repair disc". Figure 20.1 shows the window which will then appear:-

Figure 20.1 – Creating a system repair disc

Windows will ask you to choose your DVD or CD writer drive. Normally you will only have one of these drives attached to your PC, so the default option will be correct. Insert a blank CD or

DVD disc into the drive, then click on "Create disc". The disc creation process will take just a few minutes. When the process is complete, you should see the window shown in figure 20.2. Note, if an autoplay window appears, close or cancel it.

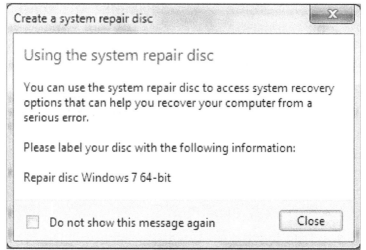

Figure 20.2 – The system repair disc has been created successfully

You should now eject the disc from your CD/DVD recorder and label it as instructed, then store it away in a safe place.

20.2 - Using the CD

To use the CD, place it in your computers CD/DVD drive and restart your computer. You may need to change the default boot device in the computers BIOS by pressing a key (usually a function key). Details of how to do this vary between computers and manufacturers. If your computer is correctly configured to boot from CD, you will see a message prompting you to "Press any key to boot from CD or DVD." Press a key on your keyboard and the CD will start, after a while Windows will start in recovery mode, just as it did in lesson 19.2 (see figure 19.4).

20.3 - Don't have a CD writer?

If your computer is equipped with a CD/DVD ROM drive but not a CD/DVD writer drive then you can still use an operating system repair CD if you get a friend to make you one on their Windows 7 machine. Note that you cannot use a repair CD created on a 64 bit version of Windows on a machine that can only run a 32 bit operating system. If in doubt, try the disc before storing it away. Better to test the disc now rather than finding it doesn't work later in an emergency.

If your computer has no CD or DVD drive at all, you could optionally purchase an external CD or DVD writer. These connect in the same way as external hard drives and are available from most computer stockists. It should also be possible to transfer the files required to run the rescue CD onto a USB stick or thumb drive. Unfortunately the details of how to do this are not currently available.

That concludes this lesson on creating rescue CD's. Don't forget to visit Top-Windows-Tutorials.com for the latest information on backup techniques and tips on keeping your data safe.

In the next lesson we will be discussing user accounts on a Windows 7 machine.

Lesson 21 – Creating And Modifying User Accounts

Windows 7 lets several users share a computer by creating separate user accounts for them. Each user will have their own personal folders on the computer and their own settings and preferences. Creating separate user accounts for all your family members is highly recommended. By creating limited accounts for your children, for example, you can prevent them changing important settings on the computer while exploring.

Even if you are the only user of your computer, if you want to take advantage of the added security benefits of running as a standard user rather than an administrator then you should create two accounts for yourself. A standard, limited account for day to day use and an administrator account for those times when you do need to change system settings. We will explain more about this in lesson 22.

21.1 - User account settings

To get started creating user accounts, open the Control Panel and then click "Add or remove user accounts". This option is circled in figure 21.1:-

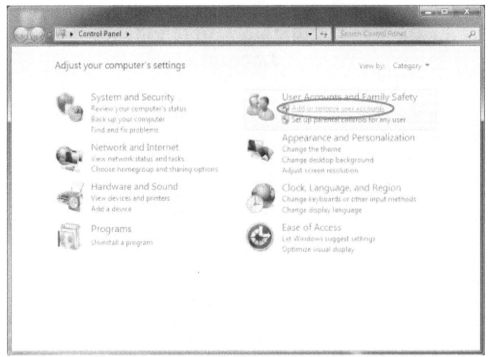

Figure 21.1 – Accessing user account options

The user accounts window will now appear, as showing in figure 21.2:-

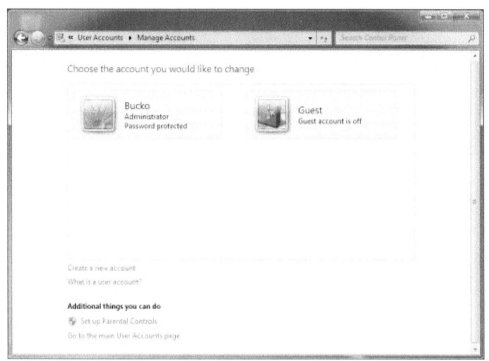

Figure 21.2 – The Manage Accounts window

21.2 - Creating a new account

Adding a new user account is easy, firstly, click on "Create a new account". You can see this option below the large rectangle in figure 21.2. Selecting this option will open the window shown in figure 21.3:-

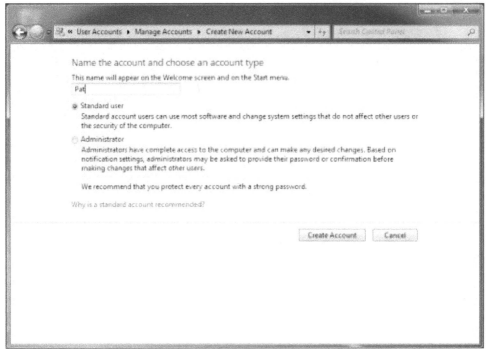

Figure 21.3 – Creating a new account

At the top of the window, enter a name for the account. This would normally be the name or nickname of the person using the account, but it can be anything you like.

Now, choose between "Standard user" account and "Administrator" account. It is important to understand the difference between these two types of account.

Administrators:- have full access to everything on the computer (including potentially the personal folders of other users) and can change any and all settings on the computer. This includes installing new software, changing networking and internet settings or storage configurations. Administrators can basically do whatever they choose.

Standard users:- Can run and use programs but usually have to ask permission from an administrator before they can change system settings or install new software. Normally, a family computer would only have one administrator, typically this would be the parent or head of the house, or the adult with the most computer experience. Everyone else, especially younger members of the family, should have standard accounts.

When you have chosen an account type, click on "Create Account". You will then be returned to the account management screen shown in figure 21.2 but with the new account in the list of user accounts.

21.3 - Avoiding administrator accounts

If you are the individual responsible for maintaining the Windows 7 PC in your home, you will need an administrator account to do so. However, running as an administrator represents a significant security risk. To take full advantage of Windows 7's improved security, create yourself two accounts, one administrator and one standard user. Use your standard user account for everyday computing and only use your administrator account when necessary. If you have already configured an account with your own preferences, first create a new administrator account and then switch your current account to a standard user account. That way you won't need to reconfigure all your account preferences for your every day use account. We show you how to switch account types in lesson 21.5.

21.4 - Creating passwords

You can optionally create passwords for all user accounts and we recommend that you do. Have your family members choose their own. For children or inexperienced users we recommend that you store their passwords securely in case they forget them. Forgetting a password will lock a user out of his or her account and therefore his or her personal folders, not good when you are trying to finish your homework! Administrator accounts can access the personal folders of other users however, one more reason not to use administrator accounts for anyone else!

To create a password for an account, click on the account in the account management window (figure 21.2). The window shown in figure 21.4 should then appear:-

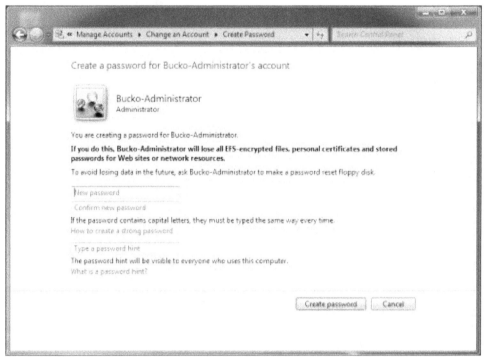

Figure 21.4 – Creating a password for a user account

Enter your chosen password in the first box, then enter it again in the box below. You need to enter your password twice like this so Windows can check for any typing errors. Optionally you can create a password hint to jog your memory. Do not make the hint too obvious as anyone with access to the computer can see it. When you have decided, click on "Create password". You will now be returned to the account management screen. The account is now password protected and the proper password will be required before anyone can use this account in future.

21.5 - Changing account types

You can easily change accounts between standard user and administrator accounts. From the account management screen (figure 21.1) click on an account and then choose "Change the account type". You will then be able to choose between Standard user and Administrator just like we did when creating a new account. Click on "Change Account Type" to confirm the changes. Of course, you will need to be an administrator in order to perform this change!

21.6 - Changing account pictures

If you do not like the picture you see for your account on the Windows logon screen (welcome screen), you can easily change it. From the account management screen (figure 21.1) click on an account and then choose "Change the picture". The window shown in figure 21.5 will then appear:-

Figure 21.5 – Changing account pictures

Choose one of the several pictures that come with Windows 7 or, by clicking "Browse for more pictures..." at the bottom of the screen, you can choose from any picture on your PC. Once you have decided, click on "Change Picture".

You can also change your account picture using the theme manager/personalization section of the Control Panel. We first visit this in lesson 29.

21.7 - Parental controls

Windows 7's parental controls are similar to those found in Windows Vista. In order for web filtering and activity monitoring to work, additional compatible software must be installed. We don't cover parental controls in this guide but we do have information on compatible software on Top-Windows-Tutorials.com. We also cover the parental controls in detail in

Windows 7 Superguide 2.

21.8 - Welcome Screen

If you create a password for your account or if you have more than one user account on your PC, you will not be automatically logged in when you start your PC. Instead, the welcome screen will show your account name and picture. To log in, simply click on your account and type your password. You can also log out at any time from the shutdown menu on the Start Menu. We covered this in lesson 2.2.

So, now you know how to configure user accounts on your Windows 7 PC and you understand the distinction between administrators and standard users. The next lesson will look at user account controls and how this helpful feature can make using standard user accounts much easier than it was in Windows XP.

Lesson 22 – The Low Down On User Account Controls

In the previous lesson we looked at how to create user accounts and discussed the security advantages of running a standard account rather than an administrator account. In this lesson we will show you how user account controls (UAC) work to make running as a limited user more convenient. Firstly, we will discuss in more detail why Microsoft implemented user account controls. In Vista, many users did not appreciate that UAC is attempting to fix a fundamental problem in the Windows security model. Instead, they berated the persistent annoying prompts that never appeared in Windows XP. In order to understand why UAC is not your enemy, we need to look at how Windows XP handled account security and why for the most part it was a failure for home users.

22.1 - Halt! Who goes there?

In the last lesson we learned that there are two different types of users on a Windows 7 machine, standard users and administrators. Generally, administrators can make changes to the computers configuration and install new software, while standard users are forbidden from making system wide changes and are only cleared to run software already installed. This security model seems fine at first glance, but what about when a standard user wants to install some new software? Certainly if you are running a family PC, it's likely that other users in the house will want to run their own software. Children might want to install games, for example.

In Windows XP and Windows 2000, if you wanted to install some new software for a standard user account, you would need to switch to an administrator account, install the software (making sure to make it available to all users), log out of your administrator account and switch back to the standard account.

This process was long winded and unfortunately it gets worse.

Lots of older, or simply badly written software just doesn't run under a standard account at all. Because of the fact that most Windows XP machines were pre-configured to run as administrator and because of the frustrations and headaches associated with running as a standard user, most Windows XP users ran administrator accounts all the time.

What is the big deal with running as an administrator? It's my computer, I can change it however I want, right? Unfortunately, running as an administrator also means that your system is wide open to attack from viruses and spyware. If you have full access to your computer, so does any program you run or accidentally run while using it, meaning that viruses can very easily propagate, hijack and sabotage key parts of your computer, often without you even knowing about it. Even with antivirus and other security software running, running as an administrator is a security risk, but running as a standard user is too inconvenient for most people, or at least it was until User Account Control was introduced.

22.2 - User Account Control to the rescue

User Account Control works in two ways, when running an administrator account, it prompts you to grant permission to make changes to the system. When running as a standard user, it allows you to temporarily elevate to administrator by entering your administrator password, thus saving you the hassle of switching accounts. Figure 22.1 shows a typical user account control prompt:-

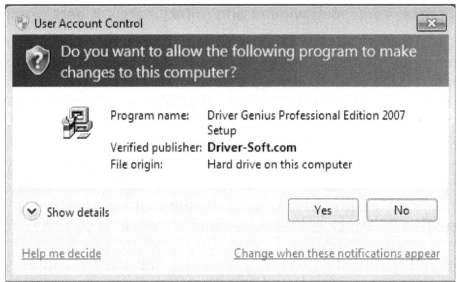

Figure 22.1 – User Account Control prompt on an administrator account

Windows has detected that a program we started wants to make changes to the computer. If this alert popped up out of the blue, you would certainly have cause for alarm. In this case it appeared because we started an installation file. Installation files are used to add new programs and features to Windows. Clicking on "Show details" will show where the program is located (the address or path of the file).

You might have noticed the shield icon, like the one on the left here, as you worked through this guide or experimented with your computer. Wherever you see this shield icon next to a task or program it indicates a task which makes changes to your computer and so may generate a UAC prompt. You may have also noticed (especially if you were a Windows Vista user) that clicking on most tasks on the control panel no longer results in a UAC prompt window appearing. Why is this? Microsoft have scaled back the amount of alerts you typically see by default on a Windows 7 machine. If you are running an administrator account then UAC prompts will not appear by default when you change Windows settings. This decision upset some security experts[1] who rightly pointed out that by doing this you are actually making Windows 7 less secure, seems like you can't please everyone.

22.3 - Changing User Account Control settings

To open the UAC settings window, open the System and Security section of the Control Panel and then choose "Change User Account Control settings" under "Action Center". Alternatively, enter "change user account control settings" into the search box on the Start Menu and click the icon that appears. Figure 22.3 shows the User Account Control settings window:-

---

1   See http://www.osnews.com/story/21499/Why_Windows_7_s_Default_UAC_Is_Insecure

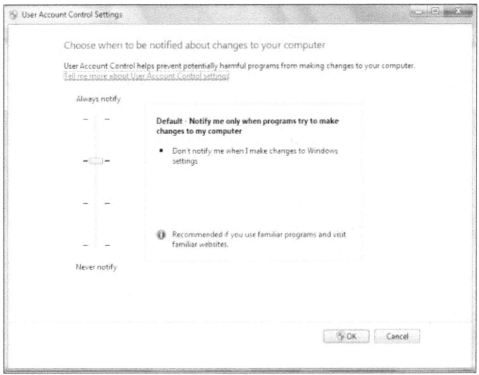

Figure 22.3 – Changing User Account Control settings

On the UAC settings window we can choose from four different settings. The settings are:-

Always notify me:- This is the highest security setting and the same behaviour as was seen in Windows Vista. With this setting, UAC asks for your permission everytime a program or a Windows system setting is changed. **To get the best security however, you must create and use a standard user account.**

Notify me only when programs try to make changes to my computer:- This is the default setting. A UAC prompt will appear when you install a new program or run a program which requires administrator access (such as a backup utility). Changing Windows settings will not generate a UAC prompt. This setting aims to balance security with convenience but some more security conscious users have speculated that malware might find a way to impersonate a Windows setting and thus bypass the UAC notification process.

Notify me only when programs try to make changes to my computer (do not dim my desktop):- This is exactly the same as the setting above, except without the screen dimming effect seen when a UAC prompt is displayed. This effect is part of a mechanism which stops malware from hijacking the UAC notification and answering for you. If your PC struggles to display the screen dimming effect, choose this setting instead of the above setting.

Never notify me:- This setting disables UAC altogether. This is not recommended.

22.4 - User Account Controls and standard accounts

As discussed at the start of this lesson, UAC really comes into its own when used with standard accounts. Windows users can finally stop using administrator accounts for day to day computing tasks and enjoy the improved security of a standard account.

Figure 22.4 shows a UAC prompt window on a standard user account:-

Figure 22.4 – User Account Control prompt on a standard user account

Notice in the picture above, we are asked for Matt's password, why is this? This user account is only a standard account and therefore does not have the necessary rights to make system changes. With UAC we can temporarily activate another account which DOES have these rights. Under Windows XP or Windows 2000, we would have to switch user accounts to make the changes and switch back again. As you can imagine, being able to immediately switch to an administrator account thanks to UAC is much more convenient.

Running as a standard user rather than an administrator is one of the best ways to improve security on your PC. Thanks to UAC, this is now possible and convenient.

That concludes this lesson on User Account Controls. This was a long lesson with a lot of theory and so give yourself a pat on the back for getting through it. We hope that you understand the advantages of limited accounts now and that you won't curse at UAC prompts quite so much in the future. The next lesson covers updating your Windows 7 machine and is not so long winded, we promise.

Lesson 23 – Updating Your PC

Keeping your Windows 7 PC up-to-date is essential if you want to stay ahead of hackers and security threats. New updates improve the security and stability of your operating system and should be applied as soon as they are available.

Note – If you still have not connected your PC to the internet, you can safely skip this lesson for now and come back to it when you get online.

23.1 - Automatic updating

Windows updates (and updates for all other operating systems) happen frequently in this highly connected digital age. When possible security vulnerabilities or other faults are found in the operating system, Microsoft issue updates to remedy the problems. To ensure that your operating system receives these updates as quickly as possible, we recommend that you enable automatic updates. To enable or check on the status of automatic updates, open the Control Panel, then choose "System and Security" and then choose "Turn automatic updating on or off" (See figure 23.1)

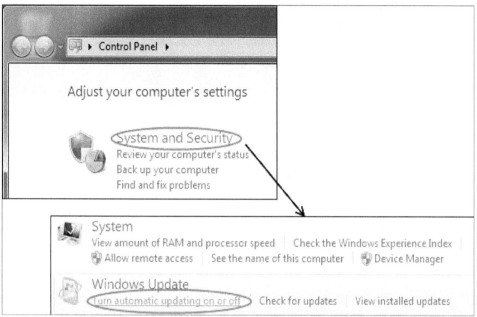

Figure 23.1 – Accessing automatic update options

The settings window for automatic updates is shown in figure 23.2:-

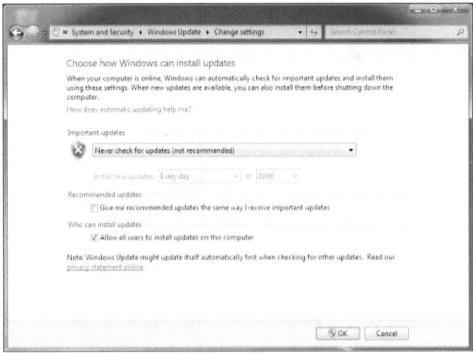

Figure 23.2 – Automatic update options

In the automatic update options window, we can choose between four different update options:-

Install updates automatically (recommended):- With this option the updating process is entirely automatic. Updates are downloaded and installed in the background. This is the option we recommend you choose. Some users disable automatic updates because they are worried about an update causing a problem with their system or some software or hardware component they have installed. While this does happen, it is uncommon. It is far more risky to leave your system without a security update.

Download updates but let me choose whether to install them:- If you prefer to check which updates are being installed before installing them, you can choose this option. Some power users prefer to do this, but for most ordinary users this is not necessary.

Check for updates but let me choose whether to download and install them:- With this option, Windows simply notifies you that there is an update available. Some users on slower internet connections prefer this option since they can postpone the downloading of updates until they are finished on the internet. Windows update is designed to download in the background and not interfere with your internet or computing session, so this option is not usually needed.

Never check for updates (not recommended):- If you choose this option, you need to manually check for updates on a regular basis. We do not recommend choosing this option.

Below the "Important updates" options there are two other options. "Give me recommended updates the same way I receive important updates" will allow Windows update to install recommend updates as well as critical updates. Recommended updates do not help protect you against hackers or malware but they do improve features of the operating system. We recommend you select this option.

The "Allow all users to install updates on this computer" option should be self explanatory if you just finished the previous two lessons. If this option is selected then all the users of this computer can install updates. Generally we would recommend this option, since updates improve the security of your system there is no reason to postpone them until your administrator logs on to the PC.

When you are done selecting update options, click on "OK".

23.2 - Manually updating

It is possible to manually check for updates at any time. It is a good idea to do this occasionally to check for any optional updates you might want to install. To get started, simply enter "windows update" into the Start Menu search box and click on the program icon. Figure 23.3 shows the window which will then

appear:-

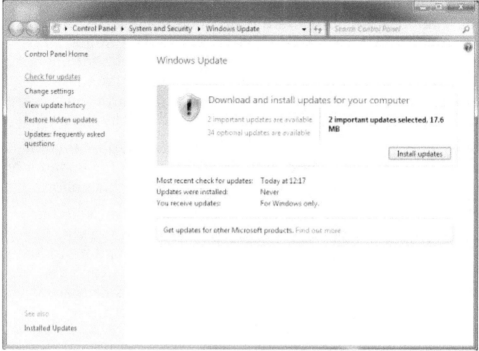

Figure 23.3 – Manually checking for updates

To check for updates from this window, click on the "Check for updates" link on the left hand side of the window. There will be a short pause while Windows connects to the internet and checks for updates. When the process is complete, Windows will notify you of any available updates. In figure 23.3 we can see that "2 important updates are available" and "32 optional updates are available". Click on either of these links to view the available updates. Figure 23.4 shows the resulting window:-

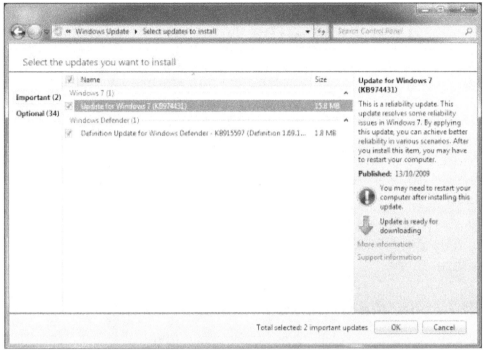

Figure 23.4 – Manually selecting updates

To toggle between important and optional updates, use the tabs on the left of the window. You should always download all the important updates, these will be selected by default. It doesn't hurt to check the optional updates occasionally too. Feel free to download any optional updates that would be useful to you.

When you are done selecting updates to download, click on "OK". The updates will then download and install.

That is all you need to know about keeping your PC up-to-date. Just two more lessons in our Windows system and security chapter now, then it's on to some more fun topics.

Lesson 24 – The Windows Firewall

The job of a firewall is to monitor and restrict the internet traffic flowing in and out of your computer. There are two types of firewall that home users typically use. Software firewalls, like the Windows 7 firewall, are programs that run on your computer. Hardware firewalls are physical items that plug between your internet connection and your PC. Typically home users will buy a router with an inbuilt firewall. We discuss this in lesson 33.3.

Note – If you still have not connected your PC to the internet, you can safely skip this lesson for now and come back to it once you are online.

24.1 - About the Windows 7 firewall

The Windows 7 firewall provides a basic level of protection against hackers and malware. To access the firewall settings, search for "windows firewall" in the Start Menu and click on the "Windows Firewall" icon that then appears (**NOT the Windows Firewall with Advanced Security icon**). Figure 24.1 shows the window that will now appear:-

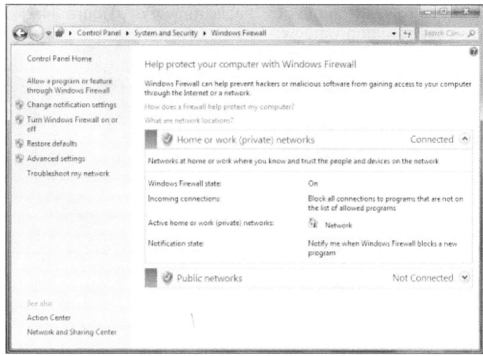

Figure 24.1 – The basic configuration window for the Windows Firewall

In Windows 7, there are three types of network configuration you might typically connect to. Home networks, work networks and public networks. To learn more about the different kinds of network, click on "What are network locations?" near the top of the window.

In figure 24.1 we can see that for "Home or work (private) networks", Windows Firewall is on (Windows Firewall state: On). We can also see that incoming connections will be blocked unless the program is on the list of allowed programs.

Our wired network, called "Network" is listed next to "Active home or work (private) networks". Looking below to "Notification state" we can see that if Windows Firewall blocks a program it will notify us.

To view settings for public networks, click on the downward

pointing arrow button next to "Public networks". Figure 24.2 shows the resulting window:-

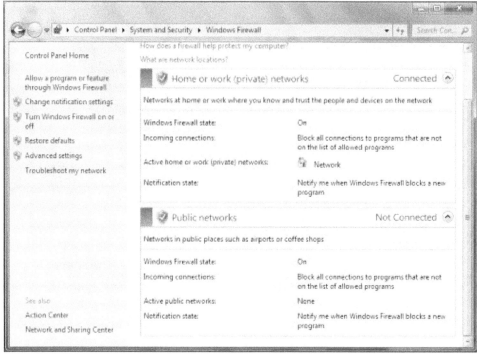

Figure 24.2 – Viewing the public network settings for Windows Firewall

By default, the basic settings for public networks are exactly the same as for private networks. One of the advantages of the Windows 7 firewall for power users is the fact that the firewall can be configured for different network connections. So, if you connect to your office via a virtual private network, but you have a network at home, you are not restricted to one firewall configuration for them both.

24.2 - Changing firewall settings

To change firewall settings, click on "Change notification

settings". Figure 24.3 shows the window which now appears.

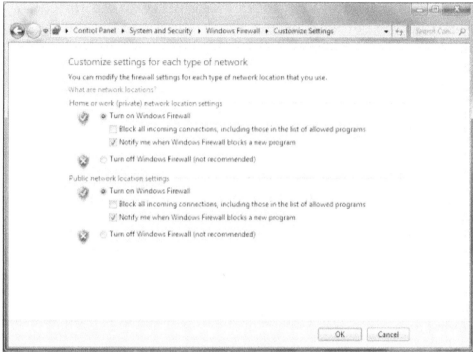

Figure 24.3 – Customizing basic firewall settings for each type of network

From this window we can tweak the firewall settings for each connection type. We might decide to block all incoming connections when we are on a public network and doing so does not affect our settings for our private network.

It is also possible to turn the Windows Firewall off entirely, by selecting the option next to the red shield icon. We do not recommend turning the firewall off unless you have a third party firewall to use instead, but it might occasionally be necessary for troubleshooting purposes.

When you are done changing settings, click on OK. You will then be returned to the previous window.

24.3 - Windows Firewall with Advanced Security

You may have noticed another icon while following this tutorial for something called **"Windows Firewall with Advanced Security"**. We can also access these advanced firewall settings simply by clicking "Advanced settings" from the options on the left in figure 24.2. The advanced settings are really only for IT experts and so we won't be covering them in this Superguide.

24.4 - Third party firewalls

The Windows 7 firewall has a few improvements over the Windows Vista firewall, but still lacks many of the features of the more advanced third party firewalls. Firewalls such as ESET Personal Firewall, Zone Alarm and Outpost firewall include individual program control and easy to configure outgoing connection protection amongst other features. Is this extra protection necessary? It is debatable, but many users prefer a third party firewall over the Windows Firewall, even in Windows 7. Figure 24.4 shows a typical third party firewall alert.

Figure 24.4 – A typical third party firewall alert message

In the picture, we can see that individual programs need to ask for access to the internet. This is true in many third party firewalls. In this system, a malicious program should be intercepted before it could send out any information from your computer. If you are considering a third party firewall, be sure to visit Top-Windows-Tutorials.com for information on our recommended firewall software packages.

That concludes our lesson on the Windows Firewall. You are becoming quite the security expert now. Next lesson we will finish our chapter on system security by discussing antivirus software.

Lesson 25 – Choosing Antivirus Software

As you use your new PC, you might have noticed the Action Centre flag in the notification area telling you that antivirus software might not be installed. Security in Windows 7 is vastly improved over older versions of Windows, but Microsoft still recommend installing antivirus software.

25.1 - What is antivirus software?

Computer viruses are computer programs, (just like everything else that runs on your PC). What makes computer viruses different however is the fact that they are designed to copy themselves throughout your computer's memory or hard drive, or even across the internet. Many computer viruses have malicious components too and may try to cause all sorts of mischief from slowing down your computer to allowing hackers to gain entry and steal confidential data.

Antivirus software is designed to watch for these particular rogue programs and stop them from running and causing whatever brand of mischief they were written for. Historically, Windows has not had the best track record when it comes to security. Windows is also the most commonly used operating system around the world and this has established it as the favourite target of computer virus designers.

25.2 - Do I need antivirus software?

While some Windows experts believe that antivirus software is unnecessary, especially if you are running limited user accounts for your day to day computing, the general opinion still seems to favour having an antivirus package installed. Antivirus software needs to scan every incoming and outgoing file on your PC, this will consume some computing time but on modern systems it is not usually noticeable.

25.3 - Choosing an antivirus package

There are dozens of antivirus packages available on the market. Some are free, others require a yearly subscription. Traditionally the free antivirus packages have provided a reasonable level of protection whereas the better paid-for solutions have had better detection rates and less of an impact on system performance. Of course, results vary widely. You can find tutorials for several recommended antivirus packages on our website at http://www.top-windows-tutorials.com/Computer-Viruses-Tutorials.html. AV Comparatives regularly test several anti virus packages, you can find their website at http://www.av-comparatives.org/

A couple of pointers to keep in mind when choosing an antivirus:-

Avoid little known antivirus packages that use flashy advertising:- There are dozens of fake antivirus packages available through the internet. These packages claim to clear viruses from your computer but actually are a huge security risk in themselves and are often exceptionally difficult to remove. Do not install antivirus software unless you are sure it is legitimate.

Expensive and popular does not always mean the best:- Two of the most popular antivirus solutions, Norton Antivirus and Mcafee have in the past been outperformed by free alternatives such as AVG or Avast.

Free is not necessarily bad:- Free antivirus packages like AVG and Avast can provide good protection. Microsoft now offer their own free antivirus called "Microsoft Security Essentials".

25.4 - Our personal recommendation

At Top-Windows-Tutorials, we do run antivirus software on our PC's. Our antivirus of choice is ESET NOD32 (or ESET Smart Security incorporating NOD32). This antivirus package has consistently performed amongst the best in the industry and has a low computer resource overhead. Visit http://www.eset.com/ to find out more.

That concludes this lesson and also this chapter on computer security. Now that your bits and bytes are secure, we can move on to more exciting topics like customizing your PC and installing new software.

Chapter 6 – Your PC Your Way

It will not be long before you want to add your own personal touch to your computer. Be it adding some new software or changing the look of the desktop. This chapter is all about making your computer uniquely yours. Yes, it is finally time to leave boring old security behind and have some fun with your new Windows 7 machine!

Lesson 26 – Customizing The Mouse

If you have been experiencing difficulty using the mouse (or touch-pad) with your Windows 7 PC, this lesson shows you some ways that you can change the behaviour of the electronic rodent in order to make it easier to use.

To get started changing mouse options, open the Start Menu and search for "mouse" and then click the icon that appears at the top. The window shown in figure 26.1 will then appear:-

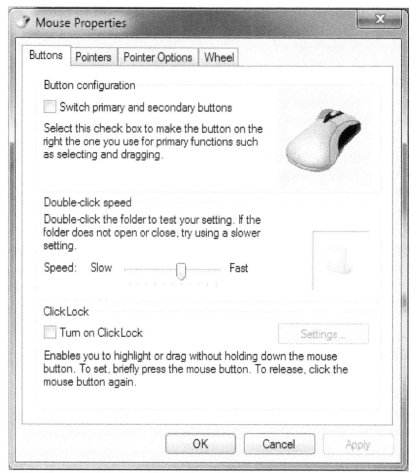

Figure 26.1 – The Mouse Properties window

26.1 - Left handed use and other button options

If you are left handed and place the mouse at the left of the keyboard, you may find it easier to switch the primary and secondary mouse buttons. This makes the mouse much easier and more natural to use if you are a left handed user. Just remember that when this guide talks about 'right clicking', it is referring to the mouse in the default configuration.

To switch primary and secondary (left and right) mouse buttons, select the box labelled "Switch primary and secondary buttons".

If you have issues with double clicking, you can change the double click speed using the sliding control in the middle of the window. If you make the double click speed too slow you may end up double clicking by accident, so be sure to try out your new setting on the practice folder on the right.

If you find dragging icons difficult, you can use "ClickLock". With this setting, you only need to hold down your mouse button for a second to "lock" it down, then hold it for a second again to release it.

Don't forget to click "Apply" when you are done changing the options.

26.2 - Pointers and pointer options

If you have difficulty seeing the mouse pointer, it is possible to choose a larger pointer scheme. Firstly, click on the "Pointers" tab at the top of the Mouse Properties window. Figure 26.2 shows the window which will now appear:-

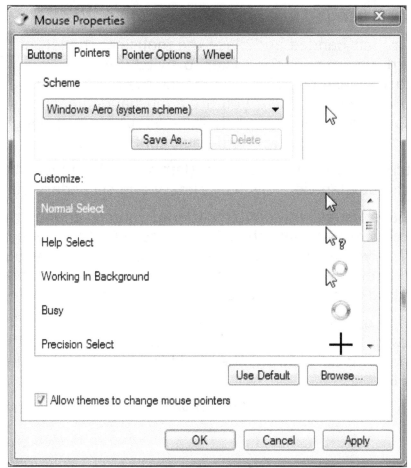

Figure 26.2 – Changing mouse pointers

Using the drop down box at the top of the window, you can choose from a range of Windows pointer schemes. Some, such as the extra large ones, are useful for people who have difficulty seeing smaller pointers.

Once you have chosen a pointer scheme, don't forget to click "Apply" to start using it. There are more pointer options you can configure on the "Pointer Options" tab. Figure 26.3 shows this tab:-

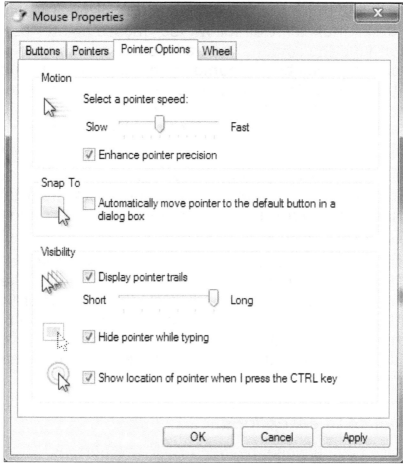

Figure 26.3 – Pointer options

If you find the mouse pointer moves across the screen too quickly, you can adjust its speed using the sliding control under "Motion" at the top of the window. Changes you make on this control take effect immediately, so you can see for yourself if the new speed is more suitable.

The "Snap To" option below the Motion control makes the mouse pointer automatically jump to buttons in windows. This can save some time but beginners usually find this confusing, so we do not recommend this.

Under visibility, there are three options. Choosing "Display pointer trails" makes a trail follow your mouse pointer as you move it around the screen. The trail looks like a gang of other mouse pointers relentlessly pursuing the pointer as it cruises around the screen. This makes it easier for some users to spot the mouse pointer as it moves. You can also change the length of the trail by using the sliding control underneath the tick/check box.

Below the pointer trails option is the "Hide pointer while typing" option, this is fairly self explanatory, if you do not want the pointer distracting you while typing, make sure this option is enabled.

If you still have trouble spotting the mouse pointer, select the option "Show location of pointer when I press the CTRL key." The CTRL or Control key is the key in the bottom left or bottom right of the keyboard. It does not matter which one you use. When this option is enabled, a circle will appear around your mouse pointer when you press Control, helping you locate it on the screen.

26.3 - Mouse wheel options

Some mice have a wheel between their two buttons. If you are using a laptop with a touch pad or a mouse without a wheel this will not be relevant to you. If your mouse has a wheel, you can alter the behaviour of the mouse wheel on the Wheel tab. Figure 26.4 shows the Wheel tab:-

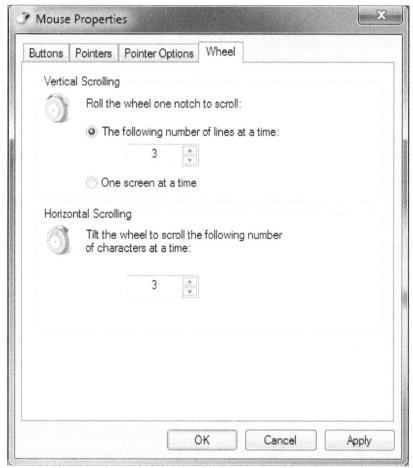

Figure 26.4 – Setting options for the mouse wheel

If your mouse has a wheel, you can use the wheel to scroll up and down text in a document or web page. By default, one click of the wheel will scroll down three lines of text.

Some mouse wheels move left to right too, though these are rare and most only go up and down. If your wheel moves left and right, you can set the amount of characters to scroll with each click by changing the value in the bottom half of the window.

That concludes our lesson on mouse properties. Hopefully, if you have been struggling to master the mouse, this lesson will have made things a little easier for you.

In the next lesson, we will discuss finding and installing new software for your Windows 7 PC.

Lesson 27 – Installing New Software

Windows 7 is compatible with a huge amount of software. Whatever you want to do on your computer, chances are there is an application out there to do it. Typically there are two ways you might purchase or acquire new software. Either on a CD or DVD disc from a retail store, or as a download from the internet. Both methods have advantages and disadvantages. Digital downloads can be very convenient, but owning a physical disc gives you a backup copy of your software and license. Many industry analysts expect digital distribution to grow and physical distribution to decline, but it may be several years before we see the end of the software store entirely.

27.1 - Choosing software

When choosing software for your Windows 7 PC, look carefully at the packaging or the website you are buying/downloading from. Look especially for the compatibility information on the packaging/website.

Software labelled as compatible with Windows 7 is guaranteed to work on your Windows 7 PC as long as your system meets the minimum hardware requirements as specified. Check the packaging or the website for details of this.

 Almost all software that is labelled as compatible with Windows Vista will work with Windows 7 though there are a few exceptions. It's worth checking on the website or asking in store before purchasing.

 Software which is labelled as compatible with Windows XP may work with Windows 7, but a significant number of titles will not work correctly or will need a compatibility update from the publisher. You may also need to use the compatibility options which we discuss in the next lesson.

Windows 7 is even compatible with *some* software designed for versions of Windows that pre-date Windows XP, though to take full advantage of Windows 7's features you should always look for a more recent version of the software if you are able to do so.

27.2 - Free software versus paid

There are a lot of fantastic free programs available on the internet, from Office applications to instant messengers and games. Many new computer users eye these freebies with suspicion. "There's no such thing as free!" or "There must be a catch!" they think. Well, a good deal of free software is both free and high quality. There are bad apples of course, software which installs spyware or other less welcome components is common. With a little research on the web you can eliminate these rogue applications and enjoy some really high quality free software. Don't forget to check Top-Windows-Tutorials.com for some great free software recommendations too.

27.3 - Installing software

Installing most software is just a matter of either inserting the disc or clicking on the downloaded file and then following the on screen prompts. When you insert a CD or DVD with a Windows program on it, the following window will usually appear:-

Figure 27.4 – Typical AutoPlay window for a DVD software title

Choose the option under "Install or run program from your media". Some titles will run directly from the CD or DVD, but most will require installation to your computers hard drive. See your products accompanying documentation for more details.

Software you download from the internet can usually be installed simply by double clicking on the downloaded program file. You need to be running an administrators account or have your administrator password available in order to install new software. Care must be taken when installing new software from the internet, as less reputable sites often lace their downloads with spyware or viruses. Files you download from the internet are stored in your downloads folder, inside your personal folder. If you are not familiar with downloading files from the internet, we cover that in the next chapter.

Every file you download will have a slightly different installation process, though there are a couple of elements that are common throughout most software. Firstly, the end user license agreement (EULA). This is a wordy, legal document which explains your legal rights when running the software:-

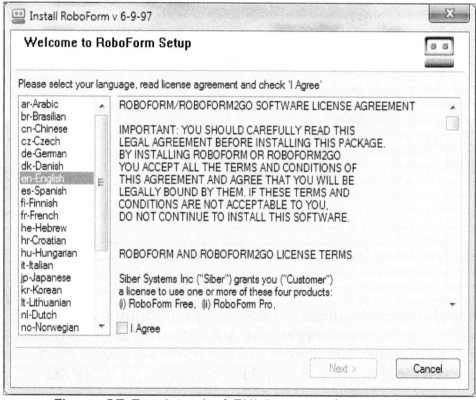

Figure 27.5 – A typical EULA, several pages long

An EULA is like the small print on a contract, we all know that we should read it but few of us do. However, you will not be able to proceed and install the software without indicating that you accept the terms and conditions in the EULA.

Most installers will also give you the option of changing the default installation directory. By default, programs will install to the program files folder on the C drive. However you can change this to be any folder on your computer if you wish. If you have used up all the space on your primary hard drive, you could install to a secondary drive for example. Usually, however, the default location is fine.

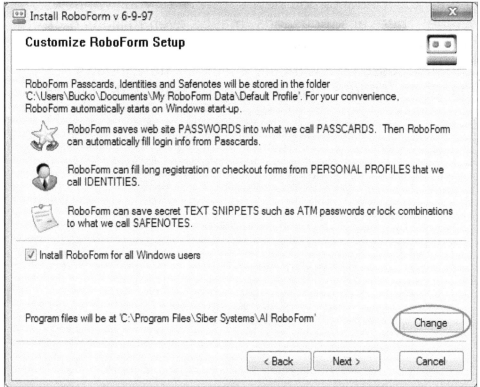

Figure 27.6 – Most software will allow you to change the default installation directory

Often, software will ask you if you want to install for all users.

You can see this option (Install RoboForm for all Windows users) in figure 27.6. If you have multiple user accounts on your system and you want to make sure that all users have access to the software, make sure that this option is selected.

When the installation process is finished, the installer will let you know. Beginners are often caught out by the progress bars or meters in installers. Frequently they indicate that the installation is 100% complete before the installation is actually finished. Do not be tempted to close the installer if it stops on 100%, wait for it to complete and close on its own. You can then start to use your new software.

You now know how to add new software to your Windows 7 machine! There are thousands, maybe even millions of useful programs for Windows machines for you to discover.

In the next lesson we will take a look at the Windows 7 compatibility options that can help run some older software.

Lesson 28 – Legacy Software And Compatibility

Operating systems, like everything else in the world of technology, keep evolving and improving. The unfortunate consequence of this is that certain older software will no longer work on more modern systems. To help with compatibility, Windows 7 has several compatibility mode options you can set for applications. This can often help older software to run on your new operating system.

Note – If you aren't having any compatibility problems with older software, you can skip this lesson.

28.1 - Windows 7 64-bit edition

Are you running a 64-bit version of your operating system? When you bought your computer or installed Windows 7, chances are you chose a 32-bit version of Windows, but 64-bit versions are becoming more common because they can utilise more memory.

64-bit versions bring about a whole new range of compatibility problems however. Early versions of Windows ran software for 16-bit processors. This refers to the largest value the processor can work with in one go. On a 16-bit machine, that number is 65535. Clearly this was not going to be adequate for long, so way back in Windows 3.11, Microsoft began to move to 32-bit. In order to maintain compatibility with the programs designed for older processors, a special compatibility layer was added.

However, when running a 64-bit version of Windows, a new compatibility layer works to ensure that 32-bit applications can run and 16-bit applications are no longer supported. Although few users need to run 16-bit Windows applications from the pre-Windows 95 days any more, unfortunately lots of installers for older games and applications were actually 16-bit applications. This means that installing legacy software on 64-bit systems can be somewhat hit and miss.

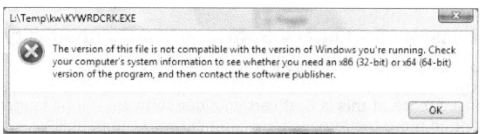

Figure 28.1 – 16-bit applications will not run on 64 bit versions of Windows

If you ever see the window shown above, you have tried to run a 16-bit application on a 64-bit operating system. No amount of setting compatibility options will help you this time.

28.2 - Using compatibility options

If you are installing software from a CD or DVD and the installation process itself is failing, you might need to configure the programs installer to run in compatibility mode. To do this, insert the CD or DVD into your computer, but cancel any autoplay prompts that appear. Now, open "Computer" from the Start Menu and locate your CD/DVD drives icon. Right click on this icon and choose "Open". Figure 28.2 shows an example:-

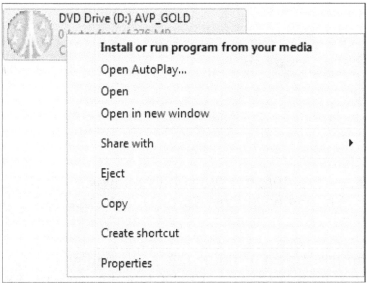

Figure 28.2 - Opening a CD/DVD to investigate the contents

Windows Explorer will now open and show the contents of the CD or DVD. In order to determine which file loads when the CD is started, we need to open a file called autorun.inf (which may appear as autorun). Locate this file in the Windows Explorer window and then right click on it. Choose "Open With..." from the context menu which then appears and then choose "Notepad" from the list of recommended programs and then click "OK". A Notepad window will then open showing the contents of the file. Figure 28.3 shows an example:-

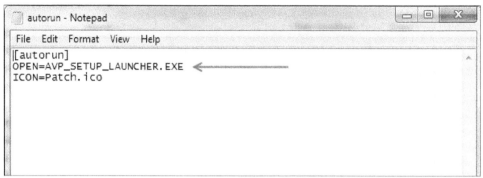

Figure 28.3 – the Autorun file shows us which file the computer opens when the CD or DVD is inserted

In the example shown in figure 28.3, we can see that the file we need to work with is called "AVP_SETUP_LAUNCHER.EXE". Find this file in the Windows Explorer window and right click on it and choose "Properties" from the context menu (just like we did when we looked at folder properties in lesson 8.1).

The file properties window will then appear, choose the "Compatibility" tab, figure 28.4 shows an example:-

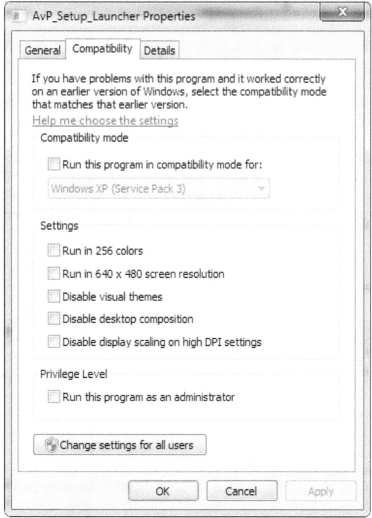

Figure 28.4 – Setting compatibility options

There are several options on this window but the most important ones are the "Run this program in compatibility mode for:" options and the "Run this program as an administrator".

When you select the box labelled "Run this program in compatibility mode for:" you can then choose the operating system the software was designed for. Check the programs packaging or instructions on the web for details of which option to choose.

Many older or badly programmed Windows programs also require that they be run as administrator. There are two ways to do this, the first way is to select the "Run this program as an administrator" option on this window. The other is to right click on a programs icon and choose "Run as administrator" from the context menu. Keep in mind that when you run a program as administrator, it gives the software full control over your PC. Never run a program as administrator unless you fully trust it. If you are running a program like this from a standard user account, you will need your administrator password every time you start it.

There are several other compatibility settings that you can try in the middle of the window, although in our experience they rarely make any difference. If your old application appears wrong or distorted when it is running then choosing some of these options may help, but experimentation is required on a case by case basis.

You can set compatibility options for any program you run or install on your PC. Sometimes software will install correctly but fail to run. To set compatibility options for software you have already installed, simply locate the programs icon (e.g by searching for it on the Start Menu) and then right click on the icon and choose "Properties...", then select the compatibility tab just like we did before.

28.3 - My software still won't run

Setting compatibility mode options will not help in every case. Some programs simply won't run on Windows 7. There are several other things you can try when faced with a program like this. Firstly, check the publisher or developers web site, if you can find it. They may have issued an update or they may sell a new, improved and fully compatible version.

If that is not an option, you may be able to use Windows XP mode. Windows XP mode is a feature available on Windows 7

Professional, Enterprise and Ultimate editions if the computer meets the special requirements of XP mode (details of these requirements can be found on the Microsoft Virtual PC web pages). When you use Windows XP mode, a window appears on your desktop with an entire copy of Windows XP inside it, running just as it would do on a normal XP PC. However, Windows XP mode is not suitable for multimedia or games software. We don't cover XP mode in this guide as it is more suited to businesses who need to run legacy applications and not home users who more typically want to run modern software, but you can find out more about it on the internet by visiting the Microsoft Virtual PC XP mode homepage (http://www.microsoft.com/windows/virtual-pc/download.aspx) or by purchasing Windows 7 Superguide 2.

There are more hints on running your legacy software on Top-Windows-Tutorials.com, visit http://www.top-windows-tutorials.com/windows-vista-compatibility.html to learn more.

That concludes this lesson on application compatibility options. In the next lesson we will show you how to personalise the look and feel of your desktop by changing your desktop backgrounds.

Lesson 29 – Changing The Desktop Background

If you are bored with that Windows logo on your desktop then it's time to change your desktop background (also called desktop wallpaper). This fun little modification has always been popular and Windows 7 makes it easier and better than ever.

29.1 - Getting started with desktop backgrounds

To get started, right click on the desktop and choose "Personalize".

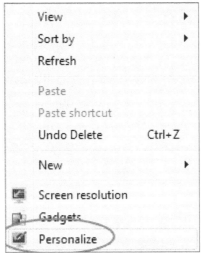

Figure 29.1 – The Personalize option is at the bottom of the context menu

The new Windows 7 theme manager will then open. See figure 29.2:-

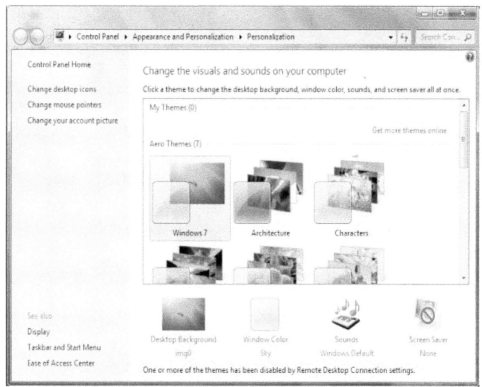

Figure 29.2 – The theme manager is under "Personalization" in the Control Panel and can also be accessed by right clicking on the desktop and choosing "Personalize"

To change desktop backgrounds, click on "Desktop Background" near the bottom left of the window. You will then be taken to the desktop background picture gallery. Figure 29.3 shows this:-

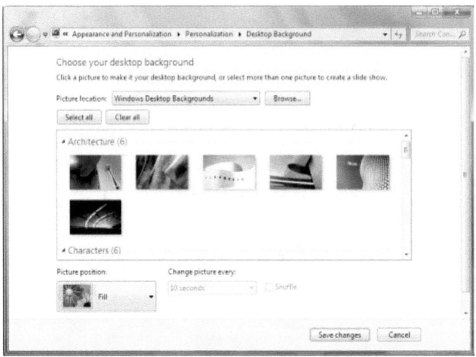

Figure 29.3 – Choosing a desktop background

Using the scroll control you can browse through a selection of pictures that come with Windows. To see what a picture looks like on the desktop, click on it once, then minimise this window if necessary. The picture should now be displayed on the desktop.

It is possible to use any picture stored on your computer as the desktop background. Near the top of the window is a drop-down box labelled "Picture location:". If a picture is in your personal pictures folder or your pictures library, simply select "Pictures Library". The gallery will now change to show pictures in your library (remember, we covered libraries way back in lesson 7). Now, choose a picture by clicking on it and it will appear on your desktop.

If for any reason you want to use a picture that is not in your picture library, you can do so by clicking the "Browse..." button and locating the picture on your computer.

29.2 - Picture positioning options

Since both pictures and desktops come in a variety of sizes, most pictures will not fit exactly into the dimensions of a desktop. To compensate for this, we can choose how the picture is displayed. There are now five different ways to adjust desktop pictures. These adjustments only affect the desktop background as it is displayed, they do not change the actual image file on your computer. You can change the picture positioning options by using the "Picture position:" drop down box, which is near the bottom left of the window. The picture positioning options are:-

Fill:- Expands the image and crops the edges if necessary, so that it fits to the current screen resolution (desktop size).

Fit:- Keeps the pictures aspect ratio (the aspect ratio of an image is its width divided by its height, if this value is ignored when resizing a picture it can become stretched or distorted). Blank space or bars are placed at the top and bottom of the image, if necessary.

Stretch:- Expands the image to cover all of your desktop. Does not always maintain aspect ratio and can make photographs look distorted or out of proportions.

Tile:- Repeats the image across your desktop in a tile pattern, this only works with images smaller than your current desktop.

Center:- Places the image in the middle of your desktop with blank space around it.

29.3 - Slideshow wallpaper

One of the neat new features of Windows 7 is its wallpaper slideshow feature. When selecting a desktop background, in the top left hand corner of the picture thumbnail, there is a small box with a tick or check mark. Selecting this box includes the picture in your slideshow. If we do that for several other pictures a custom slideshow will then be created.

By using the drop-down box under "Change picture every:" we can specify how long it takes before one image transitions to another, while selecting "Shuffle" will make the pictures appear in a random order rather than in the order we selected them in.

29.4 - Desktop backgrounds from the internet

We cover connecting to the internet in the next chapter, but if you are already connected then you may want to try this next technique. Lots of sites on the internet offer desktop wallpaper or desktop backgrounds for you to use. For this example we visited the BBC's Planet Earth website at http://www.bbc.co.uk/nature/animals/planetearth/wallpaper/ where a range of free animal themed wallpapers are available. Most websites that offer wallpaper downloads offer them in a choice of screen resolutions. You should choose the wallpaper that is closest to your screen resolution. You can find this by right clicking on the desktop and choosing "Screen resolution".

When you find a picture on the web that you want to use as your desktop background, simply right click on it and choose "Set as Background". Figure 29.4 shows this in Internet Explorer:-

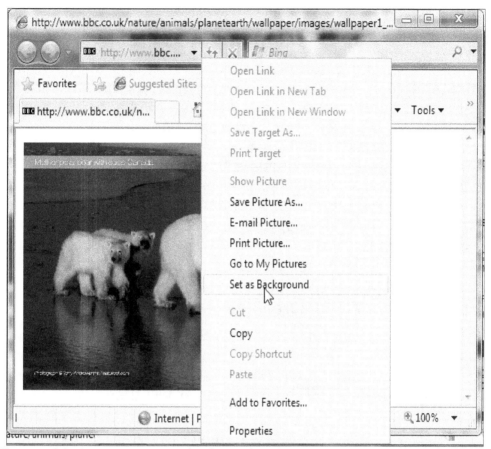

Figure 29.4 – getting a desktop background/wallpaper from the internet

Alternatively, choose "Save Picture As..." and place the picture in your pictures folder. You can then download several other pictures in the same way and create a slideshow with them.

That's all there is to changing desktop backgrounds or wallpapers in Windows 7. Give it a go yourself and have fun.

In the next lesson we look at another popular customization, screen savers.

Lesson 30 – Changing Screen Savers

A screen saver is a pattern or animation that appears on your computer screen, over the top of your windows, after a period of inactivity. Screen savers were designed to change the image on the screen to protect monitors from "burn in". This can occur when static images are left on a screen for long periods of time. On modern monitors this problem has virtually been eliminated and in these days of increased environmental awareness, monitors that are left idle for long periods of time should really be turned off. Nevertheless, many users still find the screen saver an amusing distraction, something to make a coffee break more interesting perhaps!

30.1 - Windows 7 and screen savers

Windows 7 still supports screen savers, though there aren't any enabled by default. To get started changing screen savers, right click on the desktop and choose "Personalize". Just like we did in the previous lesson. The theme manager will then open (see figure 29.2).

From the options displayed in the theme manager, choose "Screen Saver" in the bottom right corner. The following window will then appear:-

Figure 30.1 – Choosing a screen saver

Here you can choose from a range of screen savers that come with Windows. Choose one by using the drop down box in the middle of the window.

You can then see a preview of the screen saver you selected in the picture of a monitor on the top half of the window.

30.2 - Configuring screen savers

Some screen savers have extra options. For example the 3D text screen saver, which displays a message in 3D letters on your screen, can be configured to show a message of your choice. When a screen saver has extra settings like this, the "Settings..." button will become available. The settings will be different for each screen saver, figure 30.2 shows the options for the 3D text screen saver:-

Figure 30.2 – Configuring the 3D Text screen saver

To configure the message shown when the screen saver is enabled, simply edit the text in the "Custom Text:" box. Click "OK" when you are done changing settings.

To see what a screen saver looks like at full screen size, click on the "Preview" button. To exit from a screen saver, you normally just move the mouse, but on a small number of screen savers you need to press the Escape (Esc) key instead.

You can also adjust the amount of time before the screen saver starts by changing the value in the "Wait:" box. By selecting "On resume, display logon screen" you can make it so that you are required to login again when the screen saver exits. This can be useful for stopping other people using your PC while you are temporarily away from your desk.

30.3 - Downloading new screen savers

If you get bored with the screen savers that come with Windows 7, you can find new screen savers on the internet. We cover connecting to the internet in the next chapter, but if you are already connected, you may want to try out some new screen savers from the web. Be careful to download them only from reputable sites and always have an antivirus package running to avoid accidentally installing any malware.

WinCustomize.com is a great and safe site for obtaining new screen savers. For this example we downloaded a fiery screen saver from WinCustomize.com. The file was downloaded as a zip file. To use a screen saver it must first be copied outside of the zip file into a suitable location (e.g your personal documents folder). Figure 30.3 shows a typical screen saver file ready for use.

Figure 30.3 – Most screen savers are downloaded as zip files, double click a zip file to open it, then copy the contents to a suitable location

Once you copy the screen saver out of the zip folder, double clicking on it will either start an automatic installation utility or, in the case of this screen saver, it will preview it.

If you like the preview, you only have to right click the screen saver and choose "install" from the context menu. Make sure the screen saver settings window (figure 30.1) is closed before you try this. The screen saver will then be installed and selectable from your list of screen savers. To uninstall a screen saver, simply delete it from your computer.

Other screen savers you find on Wincustomize.com may install slightly differently, so check the download notes for more information. Remember that with some screen savers, you need to press the Escape key (Esc) to exit them.

You now know all you need to know to use screen savers on your Windows 7 PC.

In the next lesson we will finish off our tour of Windows 7 customizations by looking at themes.

Lesson 31 – Windows 7 Themes

Windows 7 themes let you quickly and easily customize several parts of the operating system with one quick click. Themes have been popular throughout the history of Windows, but Windows 7 drastically improves theme support. In this lesson we will show you how easy it is to use themes.

31.1 - The theme selector

You have already seen the theme selector in the previous two lessons. To access it, simply right click on the desktop and choose "Personalize". The theme selector will then appear, just like you saw in figure 29.2. We have reproduced that picture here for convenience:-

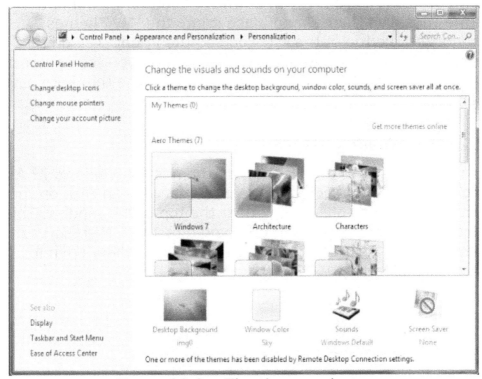

Figure 29.2 – The theme selector

In figure 29.2 we can see that the "Windows 7" theme is selected (this screen shot was taken using the pre-release copy of Windows 7, this theme was changed in the final version). To choose another theme, simply click on it.

When you change themes, you will see that the desktop wallpaper is instantly changed. Furthermore, the window colours are changed based on the theme and also the sound scheme is changed, though not all themes have associated sound schemes. Some themes have screen savers associated with them too, in which case they will be automatically applied, although the default Windows 7 schemes do not include screen savers.

You can also individually personalise the components of the theme. This is done in exactly the same way as we showed you in the previous lesson. If you do this, Windows will name the theme "unsaved theme" and place it into the "My Themes" category at the top of the list. You can then right click on this theme and choose "save theme" to save it on your computer or "save theme for sharing" if you want to send the theme to other users.

31.2 - Downloading themes

What if you want to download more themes for Windows 7? As long as you are connected to the internet, you can click on the "Get more themes online" link near the top of the window. This will open a web browser and take you directly to Microsoft's own theme gallery. Figure 31.1 shows this theme gallery open in Internet Explorer:-

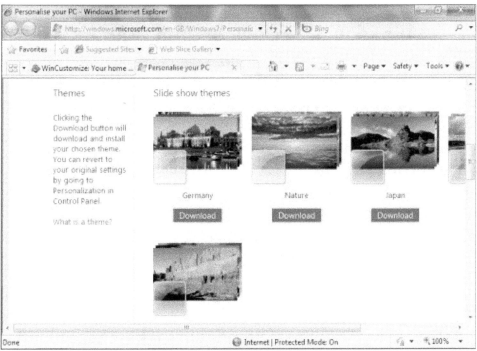

Figure 31.1 – The Microsoft Theme Gallery

Themes marked as "slide show themes" have several different wallpapers which will change automatically like a picture slide show. To download any theme just click on the "Download" button. The theme will be downloaded and applied automatically.

As time goes by, you can expect more websites to offer their own theme galleries and themepack files. If you download themes from other sites, remember to download them only from reputable sites and always have an antivirus package running to avoid accidentally installing any malware.

That concludes this lesson and our lessons on customization. If you are still hungry for more customization tips, visit http://www.top-windows-tutorials.com/Windows-skins.html where you can find out even more ways to customize your PC.

Lesson 32 – Devices And Printers

As well as great support for a huge range of software, Windows also supports a massive range of hardware too. When choosing hardware to use with your Windows 7 PC, always look for the "Certified for Windows 7" logo to ensure compatibility.

32.1 - Delving into Devices and Printers

In this lesson, we are going to take a look at the new "Devices and Printers" Control Panel section. This is a new feature of Windows 7 that aims to make it easier for users to manage hardware devices on their computers, such as printers, game controllers and monitors. To get started, open the Start Menu and search for "devices and printers" and click on the icon that appears. Figure 32.1 shows the resulting window:-

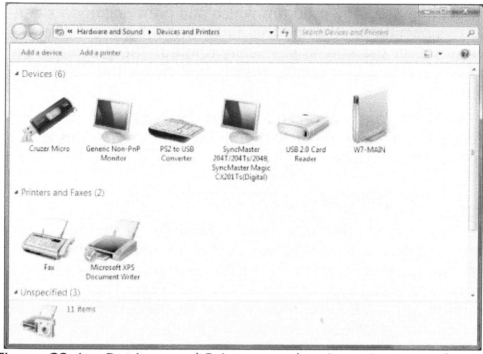

Figure 32.1 – Devices and Printers makes it easier to work with hardware

Devices and Printers gives us a very user friendly way of viewing our hardware. Your window will look different to this unless you have exactly the same hardware in your computer.

For hardware that Windows knows all about, you even get a custom icon that looks like the actual hardware device, such as the icon for the Cruzer Micro USB drive. In figure 32.1 we can also see a generic monitor, a keyboard adaptor, a Samsung SyncMaster monitor and a generic USB 2.0 card reader. The last icon in the top row represents the actual computer.

Printers and faxes are are listed on the next row. In figure 32.1 we can see the generic Windows fax machine, which requires an old fashioned telephone modem to work and the XPS Document Writer. By default, Windows comes with a printer called the "Microsoft XPS Document Writer". This is not a real printer but it can act like one. Any program which can print documents can use this pseudo printer and the document will be saved to XPS format rather than being physically printed. The green tick or check mark next to a printer means that this is the default printer.

Devices that Windows recognises but does not have detailed information on are shown at the bottom of the list, with a generic white box icon.

32.2 - Using Devices and Printers

The Devices and Printers window is great for performing common tasks with your hardware and troubleshooting hardware problems. If we right click on a device, there is a list of common actions we can take. For the Cruzer Micro for example, we can browse files or eject the device. For a monitor, we can change screen resolution.

Devices with a warning icon over them, like the Cruzer Micro in figure 32.1, potentially have a problem. This isn't always accurate as the Cruzer Micro drive was working fine, however, since there are other USB devices that are not working, Windows suspected that there might be a problem with this device.

If a hardware device has a problem you can attempt to troubleshoot it from this window. Right click on a device and choose "troubleshoot". The Windows hardware troubleshooter will then attempt to fix the problem, usually by reinstalling the drivers (drivers are software components that allow Windows to 'talk' to hardware devices). If the troubleshooter fails, you might want to check with the manufacturers for an updated driver.

That concludes our tour of the Devices and Printers section of the Control Panel and concludes this chapter. You now know how to add hardware, software and how to personalise the look of the desktop.

In the next chapter we will take you into the world of the internet and home networking.

Chapter 7 – Networking And The Internet

When the first version of Windows launched way back in the mid eighties, there were relatively few computers connected to the internet, or networks of any kind. Home computers usually sat in isolation, never talking to the outside world.

Flash forward to the modern day and millions of homes now have internet connections. Computers now talk to one another across small home networks and the web is part of many peoples daily routine. Windows 7 is well equipped to traverse the information superhighway. You already know about its beefed up security software. In this chapter we will show you how to get your PC online, how to surf the internet and also how to share files and resources in your home with some basic networking tutorials.

Lesson 33 – Choosing An ISP And Networking Hardware

Before you can take your Windows 7 PC online, you will need an internet service provider (ISP) and some hardware. Choosing an ISP depends a great deal on where you are located geographically. Deals vary widely and shopping around can often save you money. We will discuss some of the things to look for in an ISP in this lesson to help you make your decision.

33.1 - Types of internet connection

There are lots of technologies used to deliver internet connections, each with their own particular advantages and disadvantages. For domestic internet, there are four technologies that are most common. We will look at each of these technologies now and discuss the advantages and disadvantages of each.

Cable broadband:- Cable internet connections are usually considered the best way to get online. A dedicated wire which provides internet access is connected to your home and a cable modem connects between the incoming wire and your PC or your router (we discuss routers later in this lesson). Fast and reliable, cable connections are highly recommended if they are available where you live.

ADSL:- ADSL is a technology which lets phone companies provide fast internet access through regular telephone lines. ADSL connections can be as fast as dedicated cable connections in some areas. The technology is not as robust as cable but for most users it is more than adequate.

Satellite:- Satellite internet connections are available in regions where no cable or ADSL connection is available. Satellite connections can have good download speeds but have very high latency. Latency is the measure of time between sending information (such as a page request) across the internet and the request arriving at the destination. Because of their high latencies, satellite connections are not suitable for online gaming for example.

Dial up:- Dial up connections use the existing phone lines to transmit data. They are typically used where no alternative is available or the user is only a light internet user. Dial up connections are slow and have high latency but are relatively easy to set up.

33.2 - Choosing an ISP

To get the most out of the internet, we recommend choosing an ISP that provides either a cable or ADSL internet connection where possible. When choosing an ISP, do not just look for a provider that gives you the fastest speeds. Many ISP's now limit the amount of information you can access on the internet in a month or even in a day. Before signing a contract be sure to ask about download limits. On a broadband connection, it is not hard to use several gigabytes of bandwidth a month just surfing the web and watching online videos.

It is also worth checking what hardware the ISP provides with the package. If you have more than one PC in the house then you will need a router to share the internet connection between the computers (or other connected devices like games consoles). Read on to find out more about networking hardware.

33.3 - Types of internet hardware

There are lots of devices that can attach to a domestic broadband connection. Your ISP should be able to advise you on what hardware you need. We will give you a few pointers here so that you don't get confused with the techno-babble when dealing with your ISP. Some terms you will need to know about are:-

Modem:- A modem is actually a technical anachronism for the old style telephone modems that dialled up to the internet through a phone line. However, the term has been adopted to mean any device which connects to the incoming cable (or satellite). The modem then connects either to your computer, or to a router.

Router:- A router is a device that plugs into your modem (or sometimes is built into your modem). Routers share access to the internet amongst all the computers and connected devices in your home. Routers also help to keep hackers out by providing a hardware firewall, so they are recommended even for users with just one computer in the house. Generally, routers come in two types, wired and wireless.

Wired:- When we talk about networking equipment being wired, it refers to the connection used between the equipment. Wired routers connect to computers or other devices by a standard cable called an ethernet cable. Wired networks are faster, more robust, easier to configure and more secure than wireless networks. However, it is not always convenient to use wires to connect.

Wireless:- Wireless networking equipment (also known as Wi-Fi networking equipment) works without the need for cables. This makes it very convenient to use with laptop or portable computers or simply where running a wire is inconvenient. Care must be taken however to ensure that proper security measures are put into place to avoid unauthorised users stealing your internet connection or even snooping around on your computer. Wireless routers usually offer the option of connecting both wired and wireless equipment, meaning you can use the more robust wired connection where it is possible to do so and then connect other devices through Wi-Fi.

33.4 - Connecting it all up

Actually connecting all your chosen networking equipment should be straightforward, but there are so many variations and variables that it is simply not possible to go into details here.

Your chosen ISP should provide you with the instructions and technical support required to get connected. Remember that when you connect Wi-Fi equipment, you should set the security mode to WPA or WPA2 wherever possible. Do not be tempted to run your wireless connection without any security as this can leave you vulnerable to hackers and free loaders who may abuse your internet connection and even land you in legal troubles.

Windows 7 will connect to wired networks automatically as soon as you insert an ethernet cable. For wireless networks, Windows 7 will scan for networks in range and pop up a notification when networks are available. Click this notification to see a list of available networks. Figure 33.1 shows an example of a typical wireless network list:-

Figure 33.1 – A list of wireless networks in range. Beware of connecting to an unsecured wireless network

To connect to a network, simply select it from the list and then enter your network key. You only need to enter the key the first time you connect, Windows will remember it for future sessions. Remember that connecting to an unsecured network (your own or someone else's, even at a coffee shop or internet cafe) represents a significant security risk as all your web traffic can easily be intercepted by a third party.

Lesson 34 – Internet Explorer 8

Internet Explorer 8 (IE8) is the default web browser that comes bundled with Windows 7. In this lesson, we will show you the basics of starting to use IE8 to surf the web. Once you have an internet connection, the first thing most users do is try out the World Wide Web. IE8 is one way to access the web on a Windows 7 machine.

34.1 - Starting Internet Explorer 8 for the first time

To start Internet Explorer 8, either click on its icon on the Taskbar, or open the Start Menu and search for "internet explorer". Click on the icon that appears. The first time IE8 is started, the window shown in figure 34.1 will appear:-

Figure 34.1 – Setting up Internet Explorer 8 for the first time

IE8 will now take us through a few basic configuration settings for the browser, click on "Next". The window shown in figure 34.2 will then appear:-

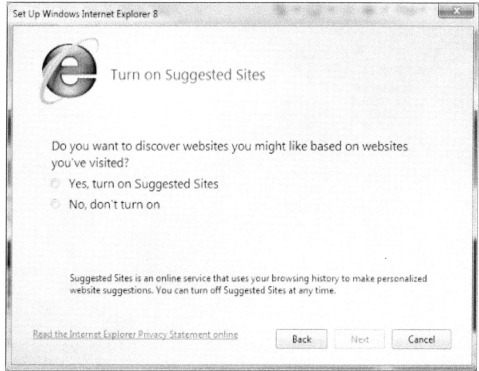

Figure 34.2 – Configuring the suggested sites option

Here, we need to decide if we want to turn on the Suggested Sites feature. Suggested Sites feeds your web browsing history into a database and then suggests other, similar sites you might like. This feature can be useful for discovering new and interesting content on the web, but many users feel that it amounts to an invasion of privacy. Make your decision by selecting either of the radio buttons, then click "Next". The window shown in figure 34.3 will then appear:-

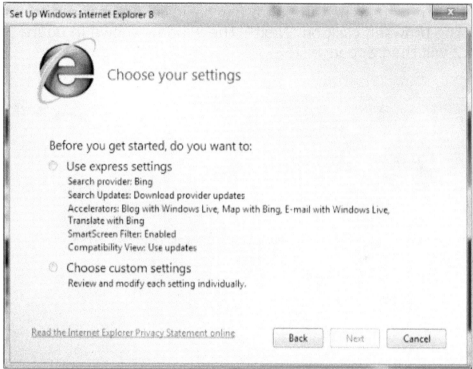

Figure 34.3 – Choose custom or express settings

This window asks us if we want to configure some advanced or custom settings or just go with the express or default settings. Users who have little or no experience using the web should choose "Use express settings". This is the setting we are using in this lesson. Once you have chosen an option, click on "Next". If you opted to use the express settings, the main Internet Explorer window will now open. Figure 34.4 shows this window.

34.2 - Your first Internet Explorer 8 session

Figure 34.4 shows the main Internet Explorer 8 window:-

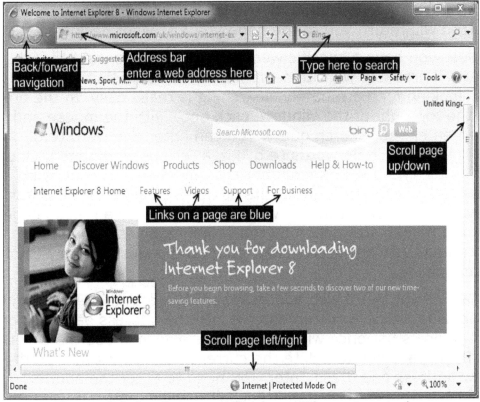

Figure 34.4 – Internet Explorer 8's main window

The first time you run IE8, you will be taken to the introductory page shown in figure 34.4. When navigating around a web page, use the scroll control on the right of the window to move up and down the page and the scroll control at the bottom of the window to move the page left and right. If the page is small enough to fit in the browser window, these controls will not be available.

Links on a web page take you to another page, links are coloured blue on most web pages. Just like in Windows 7 itself, clicking on blue text will take you to another page.

When you click a link, the back/forward navigation controls will become active. To go back to the previous page, use the back button (the arrow pointing to the left). Clicking on the forward button will return you to the page you just went back from.

Unless you have a specific web address that you want to visit, you will probably want to search the internet to find what you are looking for. Fortunately, searching is really easy. In the box at the top right of the window, click once with the mouse and then enter your search query. You can enter one word (e.g. "Pizza") or multiple words (e.g "Pizza recipes with ham"). Once you have typed your search here, either click the magnifying glass icon at the far right of the box or simply press the Enter key on your keyboard. You will then be taken to a results page, search results are ranked by the search engines own special criteria and do not necessarily reflect the pages accuracy or relevancy.

Finally, if you get a web address, perhaps from the TV or from a magazine article, you can enter it into the address bar. Click on the address bar once with your mouse and then use the Delete or Backspace key to delete the current address. Now, type the new address and press Enter. You need to enter the address exactly as given (although it doesn't usually matter if use upper case or lower case, www.MSN.com is exactly the same web address as www.msn.com).

If you entered the address accurately, you will be taken directly to that page on the internet.

That concludes this lesson. You now know enough to start using Internet Explorer 8 and exploring the internet.

In the next lesson we will look at a few other features to help make your web browsing more productive.

Lesson 35 – More On IE8

In this lesson we will finish our introductory tour of Internet Explorer 8 by looking at some other useful things you can do in the browser as you explore the web.

35.1 - Other useful IE8 controls

Figure 35.1 shows an Internet Explorer window and the features we will be looking at in this lesson:-

Figure 35.1 – More Internet Explorer features

35.2 - Tabs

Tabbed browsing is one of the most useful features to be added to modern web browsers. Tabs are useful when you want to work with two or more webpages at once, to compare prices for example. In figure 35.1 you can see two tabs currently open. To open a new tab, click on the area marked "New tab" in figure 35.1. To switch between tabs, simply click on them.

In any open tab it is possible to enter a web address into the address bar, click on the home icon to go to the "home page" (our default starting page), or start a search. Navigating or searching for pages in one tab will not change the web content displayed in another, which means you can refer back to the content in another tab at any time just by clicking on the desired tab.

You can have as many tabs open as you like, just click to the right of your last tab to open a new one. Of course, having too many open tabs at once can become confusing!

35.3 - Favorites

When you find a website you want to revisit, you do not need to remember the address, you can add it to your Favorites list instead. This is often called "bookmarking" a site. To add a site to your Favorites, simply click on the small star and arrow icon. The icon is labelled "Add current page to favorites". The page in the currently selected tab will then instantly be added to your Favorites.

To view a list of your Favorites, click on "Favorites" at the top left of the window (the button is labelled "Show favorites" in figure 35.1). You can now browse your Favorites. Figure 35.2 shows what happens when you click this button:-

Figure 35.2 – Browsing Favorites

Sites that are added as Favorites will appear under "Favourites Bar". In figure 35.2 we can see three sites in our list of Favorites.

To visit the site, just click on it once from the list and it will instantly load up. If you want to remove a site from your Favorites, right click on the site in the list and choose "Delete" from the context menu. Favorites that you delete like this are sent to the Recycle Bin and can be recovered from there if accidentally deleted.

You can also make your favourites appear as a sidebar on the left of the Internet Explorer 8 window. To do this, click on the icon labelled "Open in sidebar" in figure 35.2. Having your favourites show up as a sidebar can be convenient, if you are using a smaller screen however it may take up too much room on your monitor while you browse the web.

That concludes our tour of Internet Explorer 8. We have barely scratched the surface of what you can do with the web and with IE8, in fact we could probably make a whole new Superguide about IE8 alone! Don't forget that IE8 isn't the only way to browse, alternative browsers such as Firefox, Opera and Google Chrome have been increasing in popularity over recent years. Check them out when you become more confident, you may find you prefer them.

In the next lesson, we will finish our chapter on networking and the internet by looking at how to share files and resources around the home with Homegroups.

Lesson 36 – Homegroups

These days it is not uncommon to find two or more computers in one household. Many homes have one computer per family member. Even though the price of powerful hardware has tumbled in recent years, a computer, printer or storage device is still a significant investment for most people. Luckily, Windows now includes software that makes it really easy to share files and printers on your home network. Don't have a home network? are you sure? If you have a router that shares your internet connection between PC's in your home, either wired or wireless, then you already have a home network and you can begin this lesson. You can skip this lesson if you only have one PC in your home.

36.1 - Creating a Homegroup

To get started making a Homegroup, make sure all the family computers you want to share resources with are turned on and connected to the network (if they can access a web page then everything is good to go). Now, open the Start menu and search for "homegroup". Click on the icon that appears, the window shown in figure 36.1 will then appear:-

Figure 36.1 – Creating a Homegroup

If you have never configured a Homegroup on your network, Windows will now give you the option of creating one. Click on "Create a homegroup". The window shown in figure 36.2 will then appear:-

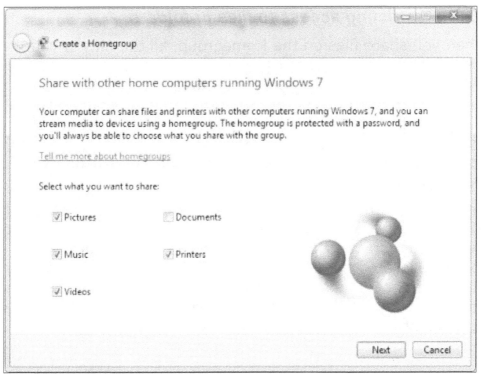

Figure 36.2 – Choosing file types to share on a Homegroup

Choose the file types you want to share on your Homegroup. By default we can share pictures, music, videos and printers. You can also share documents too if you like. If you choose the default settings then all the files in your picture, music and video libraries will be available to other users on the Homegroup. Take care not to share any personal data, we will show you how you can limit which individual files and folders you share later in this lesson. When you have decided what to share, click "Next". Windows will give you a Homegroup password, write this down exactly as it is shown on the screen. The password is 'case sensitive' which means that upper case and lower case letters are different ('A' is not the same as 'a').

When you have written down the password, click on "Finish". The Homegroup is now set up.

36.2 - Restricting access to files or folders

When you share files on the Homegroup, all the files in your libraries are shared. What if, for example, you had some video content that was not suitable for children? You could simply opt not to share videos at all, but then the children would miss out on everything. You could take the unsuitable content out of your video folder and video library and store it elsewhere, but then it won't show up when you use your video library. Fortunately there is a better solution.

Firstly, open up Windows Explorer and browse to the content you want to restrict. Note that you must browse to the folder or file on your computer directly and not via the libraries. When you have located the file or folder you want to keep private, click on it once. The toolbar at the top of the Windows Explorer window will change. Click on "share with". Figure 36.3 shows an example of this:-

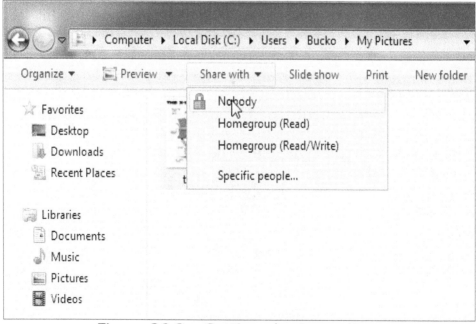

Figure 36.3 – Setting sharing options

We can exclude a file from sharing completely by choosing "Nobody", or we can give read (only) or read/write access to other users on the Homegroup. By default, other users on the Homegroup can see your files but not change them. If you need to change files from another computer choose "Read/Write", but make sure you have a backup in case someone else in the house accidentally deletes your files.

You can even choose specific people who have access to a file or folder on the Homegroup, great for keeping younger users out of content that may be unsuitable for them, for example.

36.3 - Joining an existing Homegroup

Connecting another computer to an existing Homegroup is done in exactly the same way as setting up a Homegroup in the first place. On the computer you wish to include in the Homegroup, go to "HomeGroup" on the Control Panel. You can do this by searching for "homegroup" on the Start Menu, just like we did in lesson 36.1. The window that now appears will be a little different, figure 36.4 shows the differences:-

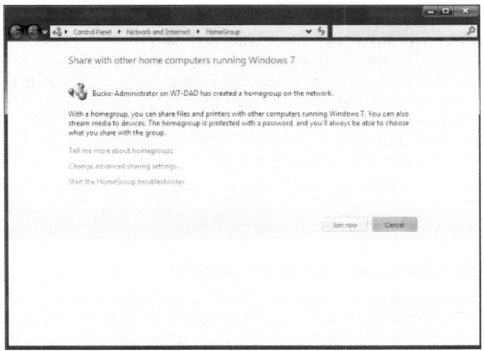

Figure 36.4 – Connecting to an existing Homegroup

This time, Windows has detected an existing Homegroup on the network. To join in and share files and printers, click on "Join now". You will then see the window shown in figure 36.2. Choose which file types to share from this computers hard drive, then click "Next".

You will then be prompted for your Homegroup password. Enter the password that you were given when setting up the Homegroup on the first PC, then click on "Next". Wait a moment while Windows searches the network. If you entered the password correctly, Windows will tell you that you have joined the Homegroup.

Note:- If you are running a third party security package that includes a firewall, you may have trouble connecting to a Homegroup. Temporarily disable your firewall and try to connect again. If you can connect with your firewall turned off, contact the vendor of your firewall product for technical support and advice or to obtain an upgrade.

36.4 - Browsing a Homegroup

You can browse a Homegroup through Windows Explorer. Simply open up a Windows Explorer window and you will see the Homegroup members in the navigation pane on the left of the window. Figure 36.5 shows an example of this:-

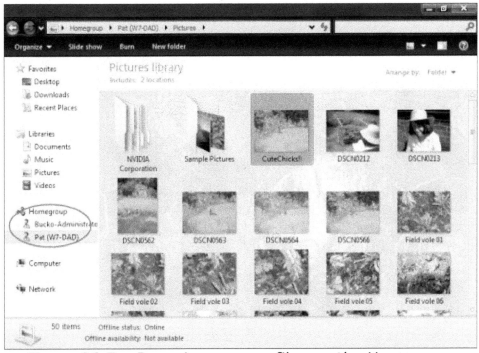

Figure 36.5 – Browsing a users files on the Homegroup

If a computer has more than one user, each user will have to log on, join the Homegroup and authorise their files to be shared before they will show up under Homegroup in Windows Explorer.

If you want to remove a computer from the Homegroup, you

can do this at any time. Open the HomeGroup Control Panel item (just like we did in lesson 36.1) and then click "Leave the homegroup..".

You have now completed this lesson on Homegroups and also this chapter on networking and the internet!

In the next chapter we take a look at some of the multimedia capabilities of Windows 7, starting with a tour of Windows Media Player.

Chapter 8 – Singing And Dancing

In this chapter, we are going to introduce you to some of the multimedia capabilities of Windows 7. Back when Windows was launched, the idea of playing videos and music on your desktop was something users could only dream of. With Windows 7, it is something you can take for granted. Windows 7 can be the centre of your multimedia world.

As well as showing you Windows Media Player, we will also take a brief look at Windows Media Center. So without further delay, let's raise the curtain on this chapter and let Media Player take centre stage.

Lesson 37 – Introducing Windows Media Player 12

In this lesson we will look at running Windows Media Player 12 for the first time. We will also show you how to play back both music and video. To get started, load Windows Media Player by clicking on its icon on the Taskbar or by opening the Start Menu and searching for "windows media player".

37.1 - Running Media Player for the first time

The very first time you run the program, you will see the window shown in figure 37.1:-

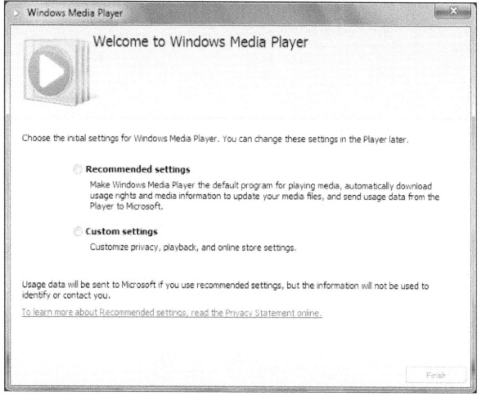

Figure 37.1 – First time setup of Windows Media Player

Windows Media Player uses your internet connection, if available, to download information about the media you are playing. Choose "Recommended settings" to get started right away or "Custom settings" if you want to analyse the settings and privacy policy in detail. For this example, we will choose the "Recommended settings" button, then click "Finish". You will then be taken to the main Windows Media Player window as shown in figure 37.2:-

Figure 37.2 – The main Windows Media Player window

Playing music and video with Windows Media Player is really easy. There are two ways to start playing a file that we will demonstrate in this lesson.

Firstly, we can drag and drop media files from Windows Explorer onto the Windows Media Player window. To do this, make sure the "Play" tab is selected, then open Windows Explorer and navigate to the folder where the media file you want to play is stored. To play a file, drag it, as if you were moving it, over from the Windows Explorer window onto the right hand side of the Windows Media Player window. The file will then play right away. Figure 37.3 illustrates this:-

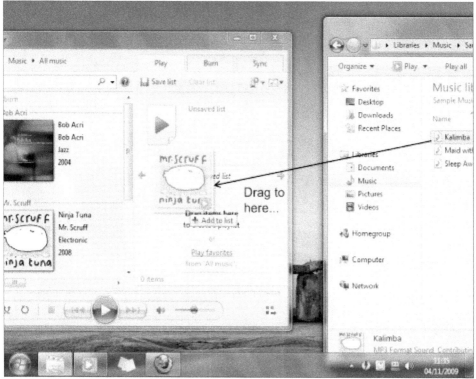

Figure 37.3 – Dragging a file to Windows Media Player

The first file you drag to Windows Media Player will start playing instantly. You can keep dragging files onto the window to create a play-list. Files on a play-list will play one after the other.

You can add video files to your play-list too, in exactly the same way. If you want to jump directly to an item on your play-list (to play it immediately), just double click on it.

37.2 - Playing video

Figure 37.4 shows Windows Media Player playing a video file:-

Figure 37.4 – Playing video in Windows Media Player 12

The picture shows the buttons available in video playback. The controls are the same when playing music (apart from the full screen control). We will take a look at each button now:-

Shuffle:- This changes the order in which files are played from your play-list. When shuffle is on, files are played in a random order.

Repeat:- Repeats the current play-list (rather than just the file you are currently playing). When this option is disabled, playback will stop when the end of the play-list is reached, otherwise it will resume from the beginning again (or a random point if shuffle is enabled).

Stop:- Stops playback of the current media file. You are then given the option of returning to the media library or resuming playback.

Previous:- Go to the previous file on your play-list.

Play:- When a file is playing, this button will pause playback. When a file is paused, pressing this button will resume playback.

Next:- Go to the next item on your play-list.

Mute:- Turns off all sound.

Volume:- Adjust the level of the volume by moving the slide control.

Fullscreen:- Make the video play back in full screen mode, taking up all the space on your monitor. Not applicable for audio files.

37.3 - The media library

Earlier in the lesson we showed you how to drag and drop media on to Windows Media Player in order to start playing it. This is handy for playing music on removable media, for example. Normally however, you would use the music library to play files from your computer. Any media files you add into your libraries will automatically be available in Windows Media Player. The media library is shown on the left of the Media Player window (see figure 37.2).

You can browse the library by file type, using the navigation pane or search for media either by name or tags by typing into the search box at the top of the window. Enter a search query then press Enter or click the magnifying glass icon at the right of the search box to start the search.

To play an item from your media library just double click it. To add it to your play-list, drag it across to the right and drop it in the same area we dropped the files from Windows Explorer.

To save a play-list, click on "Save list" then enter a name for your list. Saved play-lists appear in the library under "Playlists". You could create play-lists ready for a house party for example, or just to match your mood. To start playing a play-list, just double click it.

That concludes this lesson on Windows Media Player. Now you know how to play audio and video media files.

In the next lesson we will look at how to copy your CD collection to your computer and create a digital jukebox of all your favourite tunes.

Lesson 38 – Ripping CD's

Have you ever wanted to create your own jukebox? By ripping your CD's to your computers hard drive you can do just that. Ripping a CD means taking a copy of the music on the CD and storing it to your computer. The copyright law in most countries allows you to do this, as long as you own a copy of the original CD. This means that you can access all your music without having to have the original CD in the CD drive or player!

38.1 - Setting ripping options

Before we get started ripping CD's, let us take a look at some options. Click on "Organize" and then choose "Options". Now, choose the "Rip music" tab. Figure 38.1 shows you how to do this:-

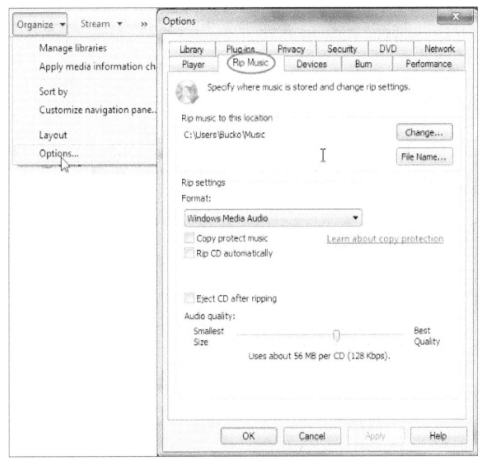

Figure 38.1 – Accessing ripping options

By default, music that you rip will be stored in Windows Media Audio format. If you are planning to use the music on a generic MP3 player, it might not be compatible with Windows Media Audio format. Choose "Mp3" in that case. You can change formats by using the drop down box under "Format:". If you are playing the music files back on high quality audio equipment, you may also want to up the quality of the copy, though doing so increases the file size. You can change quality settings by using the slide control at the bottom of the window. There is no right or wrong setting, experiment and find out what sounds best to you.

When you are done setting ripping options, click on "Apply" then on "OK". You will then be taken back to the main Media Player window.

38.2 - Ripping a CD

To rip a CD using Windows Media Player 12, firstly insert your audio CD. It should then show up in the navigation pane, under "Music". Click on it once. Figure 38.2 shows a Media Player Window with an Audio CD ready to play:-

Figure 38.2 – An audio CD in Windows Media Player

Just like regular media, you can double click on audio tracks to play them. You can also drag them over to the right (as long as the Play tab is selected) and make a play-list.

We could start ripping the CD right away, but if we did, the files would not be correctly named. To save the hassle of renaming them later, you can look up the track names in the online CD database. To do this, right click on the CD's icon in the media library (in figure 38.2 the icon is called "Unknown album 04") then choose "Find album info" on the context menu that appears. Media Player will then connect to the internet and look up the track names and information about the album. This saves you entering them manually later. Of course, you will need an internet connection for this to work. Figure 38.3 shows the "find album information" window:-

Figure 38.3 – Looking up an album online

Sometimes Windows Media Player will find the album information automatically, other times you will need to search for it yourself by entering the artist and album name into the search box. When you find a match for the album, click on it from the list and then click "Next". You will be able to confirm that the details are correct before clicking on "Finish".

The track listing will then be automatically filled out, just like in figure 38.4:-

Figure 38.4 – Filling out track names by looking them up on the internet is much quicker than typing them yourself

We are now ready to start ripping some music. You can rip the entire CD or individual tracks, just deselect the ones you don't want. When you are ready to start ripping the disc, right click on the disc icon in the library pane (it will now be correctly named if you looked it up online) and choose "Rip CD to library".

38.3 - Copy protection options

If this is the first time you have ripped a CD, the window shown in figure 38.5 will appear:-

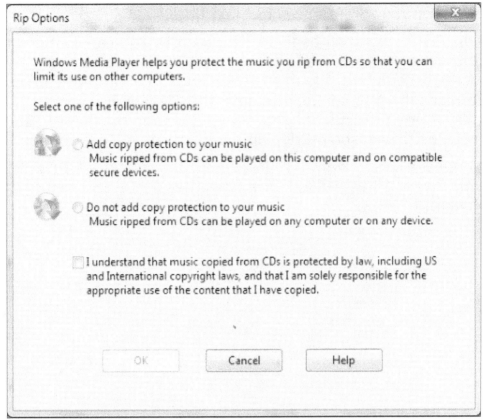

Figure 38.5 – Setting copy protection options

When ripping music from CD's, you can choose to add protection to your ripped audio files. Adding protection can help you use the media within copyright law, but it can also cause problems with some types of media players, so we recommend that you do not. You must also tick/check the box at the bottom of the window that states that you understand most music CD's are protected by copyright law. Please use the files you copy/rip from your CD's for your own personal use and do not share them with friends or on the internet.

Click on "OK" when you have selected an option and ticked/checked the box. Ripping will then begin. This window will only appear the first time you rip a CD, Media Player will remember your preferences for next time.

Media Player will then begin ripping the CD. You can continue to use the program while this takes place. When the ripping process is complete, the music files will be added to the library automatically. You can now remove the CD and enjoy your music at any time just by accessing it through the library. That concludes this lesson on ripping audio tracks in Media Player 12.

In the next lesson we will round up our introductory tour of Media Player 12 as we look at a few other useful features of the software.

Lesson 39 – Wrapping Up Media Player

In this lesson we will be going over some of the features we briefly mentioned in the other lessons, especially the media library and play-lists.

39.1 - Browsing libraries

As we mentioned in lesson 37, the libraries in Windows Media Player 12 and your music library are linked, meaning you can browse your music collection from Windows Explorer or through Media Player. Browsing in Media Player can be more convenient if you want to play and browse music and video.

Just like in Windows Explorer, there are different views you can choose for browsing your media. If you do not like how the data is laid out in your media library, you have several options. Use the drop down box next to the search box to change views. Figure 39.1 shows where this control is:-

Figure 39.1 – The view options control

Depending on what type of media you are viewing, you will have several choices. Details view is useful for working with lots of tracks at once. In this view, you can set ratings by simply clicking on the stars next to the song title. Figure 39.2 shows a

media library viewed in details view:-

Figure 39.2 – Media library in details view

Using the scroll control near the bottom of the window it is possible to see other columns which contain various information about your music or media files. To sort by a column, click the column once.

By right clicking on a column and choosing "Choose columns" it is possible to see a list of all the different types of information that can be displayed about the media files. Figure 39.3 shows this list:-

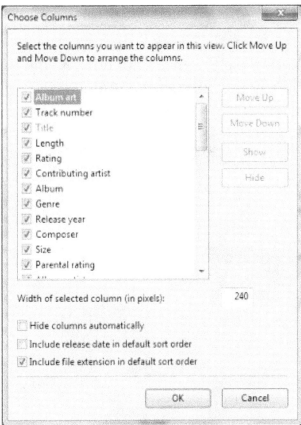

Figure 39.3 – Choosing columns to display in the media library

Of course, some categories will not be relevant to all types of media. To display a column, simply select it then click "OK", it will then appear.

You can also resize columns by dragging them, or reorder columns by dragging them to a new place. As you can see, working with Media Player is a lot like working with Windows Explorer. Don't forget there is also a very handy "Search" box, where you can search by artist, album or song title. This is very useful for quickly finding things in your media library.

39.2 - Viewing pictures

We have talked about video and music files in Media Player but we did not mention picture files until now. Media Player 12 can view picture files too. Figure 39.4 shows the picture section of the media library:-

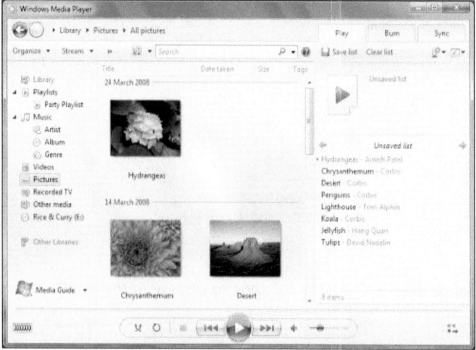

Figure 39.4 – Browsing pictures in Windows Media Player

To view pictures, just double click on them, Windows Media Player will play them as a slideshow. You can queue pictures up in a play-list just like other media, making it easy to create a custom slide show.

That concludes our tour of Windows Media Player 12. We have barely scratched the surface of the power of Windows Media Player in these lessons, do not be afraid to dive in and experiment, it is the best way to learn.

In the next lesson we will take a brief tour of another multimedia program in Windows 7, Windows Media Center.

Lesson 40 – Windows Media Center

In this lesson we are going to have a brief look at Windows Media Center. We will learn what Media Center is all about and what it can do for you.

40.1 - What is Windows Media Center?

We have seen that Windows is great for browsing and viewing media files. Windows Media Center takes this functionality out of the study and into the living room. If you ever hook your PC up to a big screen TV, you may want to use Media Center to explore your media. Let us start the program and look at a screen shot to show you what we mean. You can start the program by searching for "Windows Media Center" on the Start Menu and then clicking the icon that appears. Figure 40.1 shows the Windows Media Center welcome screen:-

Figure 40.1 – Welcome to Windows Media Center

When Media Center is launched for the first time, this is the screen we will see. "The best way to experience TV on your PC" says the text. That may be true if you have the correct hardware, if not, Media Center is still a great way to experience the PC on your TV! To get started, click on "Continue". Just like in Media Player and Internet Explorer, you will then be given the option of choosing the express setup or the custom setup. We will go with express for this lesson. You will now be on the main Media Center interface. Figure 40.2 shows this:-

Figure 40.2 – The main Media Center interface

The main Media Center interface is designed to work with a remote control and run at full screen on a TV set. You can also use the keyboard or mouse if you prefer. Click on an item or use the up and down arrow keys to navigate around.

Figure 40.3 shows the Pictures + Videos module, you can use this for browsing through your pictures and videos while sitting on the couch, appropriate hardware permitting of course:-

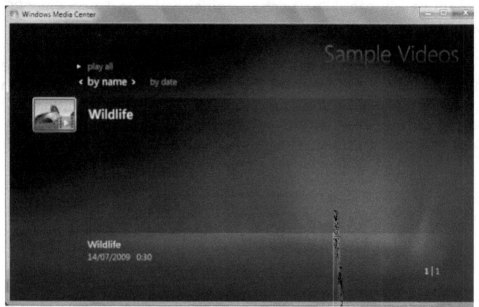

Figure 40.3 – Browsing video files

Although we only have one video in the library, you can see that it has been given a large icon that would be easy to see sitting back on the couch. To play a video, simply select it with your remote control, keyboard or mouse. Figure 40.4 shows the "Wildlife" video playing in Media Center:-

Figure 40.4 – Playing a video in Media Center

The controls for stopping and starting the video are similar to those in Windows Media Player, but the interface is redesigned for home theatre PC use. To exit the video player and go back to the main menu, use the back button in the top left hand corner of the screen.

You can also enjoy music from the Media Center interface, just select "Music" from the main menu. You can then open your music library and browse by category or use search to search for a particular song or artist. While a song plays, you can browse the rest of Media Center too. It is even possible to rip a CD directly from the Media Center interface.

That concludes our brief look at Windows Media Center. While Windows Media Center will not be of use to everyone, for some of you we hope that this little tour has inspired you to learn more. If you are interested in learning more about using Media Center with your High Definition TV and a remote control, there are plenty of resources available online. Start with the official

Microsoft page (http://www.microsoft.com/windows/windows-media-center/get-started/default.aspx) and have fun!

That concludes our chapter on multimedia in Windows 7. The next chapter focuses on routine PC maintenance and troubleshooting, to help keep your new PC running in tip-top condition.

Chapter 9 – Troubleshooting And Maintenance

Your PC is almost certainly the most versatile gadget you have in your home. No normal television, toaster or microwave oven could ever come close to performing as many tasks as even the most humble Windows 7 PC. This is great of course, but the downside is that PC's typically need more maintenance than regular household gadgets. Don't worry if that sounds like hard work, if you followed our advice on PC security then hopefully you won't encounter too many problems. In this chapter we will show you some simple things you can do to keep your Windows 7 machine running like new.

Lesson 41 – Uninstalling Software

If you no longer use a program, it is a good idea to uninstall it. Uninstalling software frees up disk space and can free up computer resources too if the software in question was running all the time. Often it is necessary to uninstall an old program to make way for a new one. This is true in the case of most security software (i.e firewall and antivirus packages). Sometimes, it is a good idea to uninstall and reinstall a program if you are experiencing technical problems with it.

41.1 - An example uninstallation

In this example, we are going to look at how we uninstall Eset Smart Security. The actual uninstallation process will be different for every piece of software but the basic steps are usually the same. Since Eset Smart Security is a security product, uninstalling it can be more complex than other, more simple software, so it makes a good example.

Before you begin uninstalling any software, it is a good idea to make sure it is not running. Although a properly written uninstall script should take care of this, it never hurts to check yourself. If you do not see a window for your program, check the notification area (see lesson 14) for the programs icon. If you can see an icon, right click on it and choose "quit", "close" or "shutdown" if the option is available. In the case of ESET Smart Security, there is no shutdown option, so hopefully the uninstaller will take care of that for us.

To start the uninstallation process, open the Control Panel and choose "Uninstall a program" from the bottom left. Figure 41.1 shows the correct icon:-

Figure 41.1 – The Uninstall option on the Control Panel

Windows will now show you a list of all the programs installed on your PC. You may need to Scroll down until you find the program you want to uninstall. Then click on it and choose "uninstall" if the option is available or "change" if it is not. Figure 41.2 shows an example of this:-

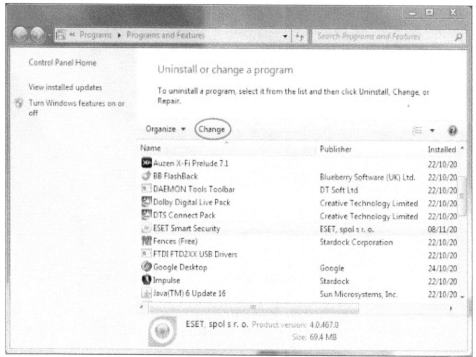

Figure 41.2 – Choosing a program to uninstall. Some software must be uninstalled by selecting "Change" while other software will have an "Uninstall" option in the same place

Once you click on "Uninstall" or "Change" the uninstallation process will begin, you should then follow the on screen prompts to remove your software. These prompts will be slightly different for every program you uninstall, but they are usually straightforward. Normally you will need to confirm that you want to remove the software when User Account Control prompts you.

Sometimes you will have to restart your PC to finish the uninstallation process. The uninstaller should offer to do this for you if it is necessary. Once your computer restarts, the uninstallation process is complete. That concludes this short lesson on uninstalling software.

In the next lesson we will take a look at how to remove temporary files and other clutter using the Disk Cleanup utility.

Lesson 42 – The Disk Cleanup Utility

In Windows 7 you can reclaim disk space and clean up temporary internet files by using the Disk Cleanup Tool. This tool was present in Windows XP and Windows Vista too, but it has been improved in Windows 7.

42.1 - Starting a disk cleanup

To start the tool, click the Start globe, and enter "Disk Cleanup" in the search box, then click on the icon that appears. Notice the spelling of "disk" with a 'k'. When talking about hard disks, Windows always spells them with a 'k', probably for historical reasons.

Once you click on the Disk Cleanup icon, The window shown in figure 42.1 will then appear:-

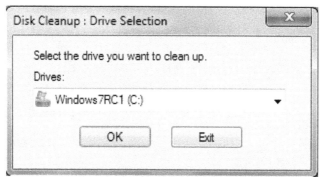

Figure 42.1 – Choosing a disk to clean up

Choose a drive to clean up by using the drop-down box control. Most computers will only have the C: drive, but some may have more. In this lesson we will show you how to clean the C: drive, which is usually the drive or partition that Windows is installed to. Choose the C: drive (it should be selected by default) then click "OK".

42.2 - Choosing cleaning options

The Disk Cleanup utility will then scan for temporary files. When this process is complete, the window shown in figure 42.2 will appear:-

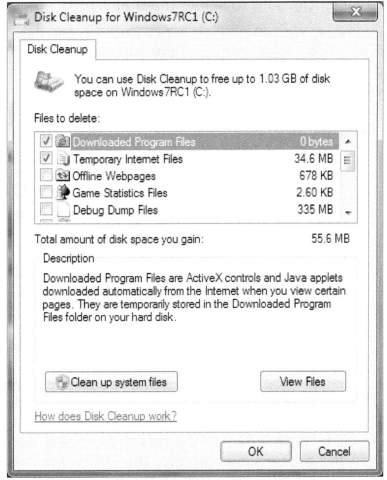

Figure 42.2 – Choosing temporary files to remove

Figure 42.2 shows the Disk Cleanup utility presenting us with a list of all the temporary files that can be deleted from the computer. If you scroll down the list and click on an item, you can see a description of the files that this cleanup option removes. In figure 42.2, the "Downloaded Program Files" option is selected, in the description we can see that this includes ActiveX and Java applets downloaded automatically. Selecting this option will not delete files you have downloaded into your downloads folder. Generally, since each option only cleans temporary files, it is safe to select them all.

For this example, we will choose every item on the list, then click on "OK". The Disk Cleanup utility will then ask us to confirm that we want to delete the files, figure 42.3 shows the window which will appear:-

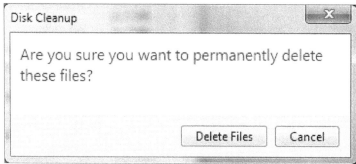

Figure 42.3 – Confirm the removal of temporary files to start the cleanup process

This is your last chance before the items are deleted. Unless there is something you really wanted to recover from the Recycle Bin or from the temporary files or error logs on your PC, it is safe to click "Delete Files". The cleanup process will then begin. When the process is complete, the utility will exit automatically. You have now cleaned the temporary files from your computer and reclaimed the disk space.

That concludes this lesson on the Disk Cleanup utility. PC maintenance really isn't as difficult as you imagined is it?

In the next lesson we take a look at how we can improve system performance with the disk defragmenter tool.

Lesson 43 – Disk Defragmentation

As you go about your daily computing routine, adding files, removing files and rearranging files, the hard disk in your computer becomes more and more fragmented. File system fragmentation slows down access to files because the pieces of a file may be scattered across the disk, rather than stored together neatly. To combat this problem, the Disk Defragmenter tool can automatically rearrange your hard disk. The tool is easy to use and completely safe and will even run automatically when configured.

43.1 - The Disk Defragmenter window

To start the Disk Defragmenter, open the Start Menu and search for "disk defragmenter", then click on the icon to load the program. The window shown in figure 43.1 will then appear:-

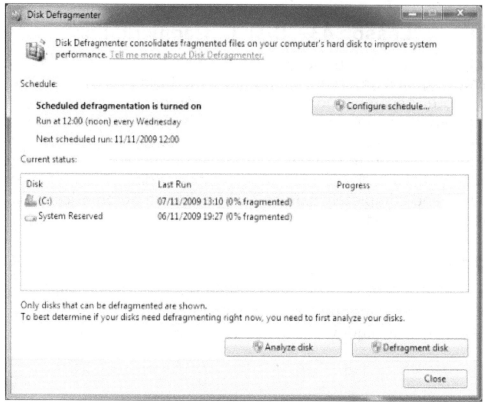

Figure 43.1 – The Disk Defragmenter tool

Figure 43.1 shows the main Disk Defragmenter tool window. From this window we can schedule regular defragmentation or manually defragment any hard disks in our computer. We will take a look at scheduled defragmentation first. Clicking on "Configure schedule..." will open the window shown in figure 43.2:-

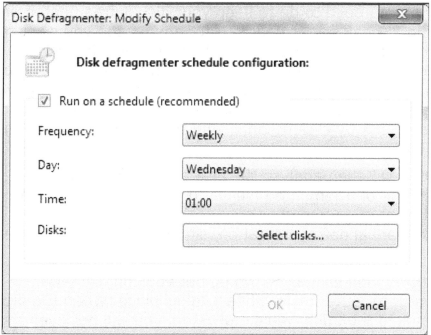

Figure 43.2 – Scheduling a defragmentation

43.2 - Setting a schedule

In this window we can choose a schedule for automatic "set it and forget it" disk defragmentation. Choose a time when your computer is likely to be on, but not doing anything too intensive. If like most people you turn your computer off at night, the default time of 1AM is not suitable, so choose another time instead. By changing the "Frequency:" control, you can also choose between daily, weekly or monthly defragmentation. Daily is a little excessive but monthly might be suitable for a computer that isn't used frequently. Weekly will be the best option for most users. Click on "OK" when you are done setting the schedule. You will then be returned to the main Disk Defragmenter window as shown in figure 43.1.

43.3 - Manual defragmentation

Once you have set a schedule for disk defragmentation, that is really all you need to do to keep your disk defragmented and working at peak performance. If for any reason you want to do a manual disk defragment then simply choose the disk to defragment from the list in the middle of the window (in figure 43.1). Most systems will only have a C: drive and probably not the "system reserved" drive that we can see in figure 43.1. Choose a disk by clicking on it and then click on the "Analyze disk" button.

Windows will then analyse the disk and tell you what the percentage of fragmented files is. If this value is high, you might want to go ahead and manually defragment the disk. To start a manual defragmentation, simply click on "Defragment Disk".

Degragmenting will take a while, but you can use your computer for other tasks while it takes place. When the process is complete the utility will simply stop, you will not even be notified that it is done!

That is all there is to keeping your disks defragmented with the Disk Defragmenter utility.

In our next lesson, we will look at the System Restore utility. This utility can help solve serious computer problems by restoring your system settings to an earlier time.

Lesson 44 – System Restore Utility

The System Restore utility was introduced with Windows XP and has been refined in Windows Vista and in Windows 7. If you have a serious problem with your PC after installing a new program or piece of hardware, the System Restore utility can "roll back" to an earlier time when your PC was working correctly.

44.1 - Starting a System Restore

To start the utility, open up the Start Menu, and search for "system restore" and click the icon that appears at the top. The window shown in figure 44.1 will then appear after a short delay:-

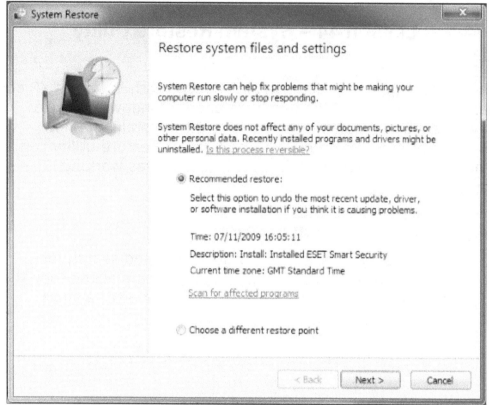
Figure 44.1 – The System Restore wizard

The System Restore 'wizard' will now start and guide you through the process. Unlike restoring an image backup (see lesson 18) System Restore only affects system settings. Files such as pictures, videos and e-mails will not be altered. Because of this it is more convenient to use System Restore than it is to restore from an image backup when troubleshooting computer problems.

44.2 - Choosing a restore point

The System Restore utility will give us two options on the first window. "Recommended restore:" or "Choose a different restore point". The recommended restore will restore from the most recent restore point. This is the option that we use in this lesson. If you restore from the recommended restore point and your system still malfunctions, you can choose a different, earlier restore point. Figure 44.2 shows the window that appears if you select "Choose a different restore point":-

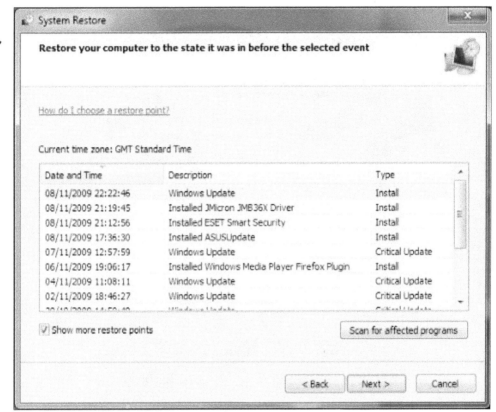

Figure 44.2 – Choosing a restore point

To choose a restore point, simply select it from the list and then click on "Next >". You can see a description of why the restore point was created, along with the date and time it was made. If you suspect that the problems you are having are down to a specific program or update you installed, you can restore to a specific restore point to test your theory.

44.3 - Restoring from a restore point

Once you choose a system restore point, you will need to confirm your selection, figure 44.3 shows the window that appears:-

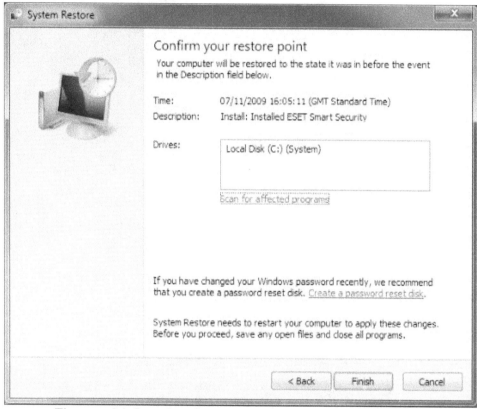

Figure 44.3 – Confirming a system restore point

This window gives us some pointers to note before we begin with the system restore process. We can "Scan for affected programs" to see if any of the programs on our computer are likely to need reinstalling after this process is completed. If you have recently changed your password, using System Restore might revert back to the old password, so make sure you can remember them both or create a password reset disk.

Since the restore process will restart your PC, you also need to close down any running programs and save your work. Click on "Finish" when you are ready to proceed.

You will receive one final warning not to interrupt the system restore process, click on "Yes" and the process will then begin. It will take several minutes to complete.

When the process is complete, the system will restart and return you to the welcome screen. When you log back into your computer, you should see the window shown in figure 44.4:-

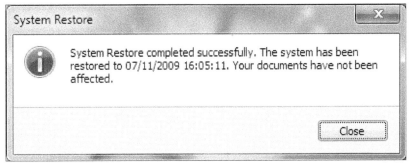

Figure 44.4 – System restore completed successfully

Click on "Close". You should now check to see if the problems you were having are resolved. If they are not, you can start System Restore again and either undo the system restore or choose another restore point.

44.4 - Undoing a system restore

Before the System Restore utility rolls back to a restore point, it creates a restore point containing your current configuration. That means you can easily undo a system restore. Start the System Restore utility again and the window shown in figure 44.5 should appear:-

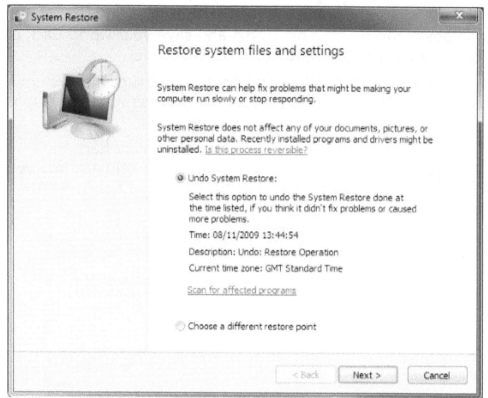

Figure 44.5 – Undoing a system restore is easy

When you choose "Undo System Restore:" the process works in exactly the same way as when you use system restore normally. You are in actual fact restoring from a restore point that was created before you ran System Restore the first time!

44.5 - Creating your own system restore point

Users can easily create their own system restore point at any time. To do this, open the Start Menu and search for "system restore" but this time, choose "Create a restore point" from the Start Menu. The window shown in figure 44.6 will then appear:-

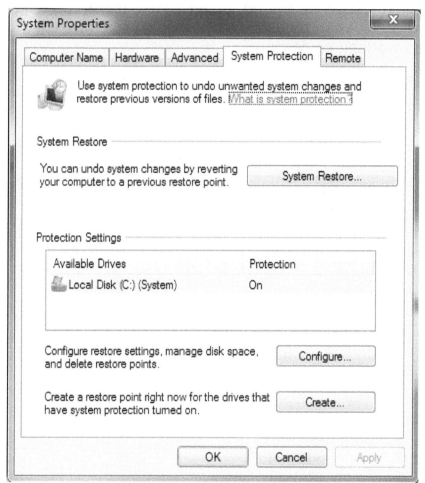

Figure 44.6 – Creating a system restore point is easy

All that you need to do to create a system restore point is choose a drive from the list in the middle of the window. Usually there is only the one drive, C:, where Windows is installed. Choose the C: drive and then click on "Create...". Windows will prompt you to name your restore point. Enter any name you like and click "Create" again. Wait a moment until Windows tells you that the restore point was created. You can now close the window and use System Restore to roll back to this point if necessary.

In the next lesson we will be taking a look at the Task Manager. This handy tool can be used to close down software which has stopped working correctly.

Lesson 45 – The Task Manager

Sometimes when you work with your computer, an application will stop responding to the mouse or keyboard. When this happens, it will not be possible to close the program because the window will freeze, preventing you from doing anything with it. For (hopefully rare) situations like these, you can use the Task Manager to force the application to close.

45.1 - Starting the Task Manager

You can start the Task Manager in two ways. The first way is to open the Start Menu and search for "taskmgr" and then click on the icon that appears at the top, Task Manager will then open.

If your computer is not responding normally, you may not be able to open the Start Menu at all. In that case, use the following keyboard shortcut. Press and hold the Control, Alt and Delete keys together.

When you press these three keys together, the screen shown in figure 45.2 will then appear:-

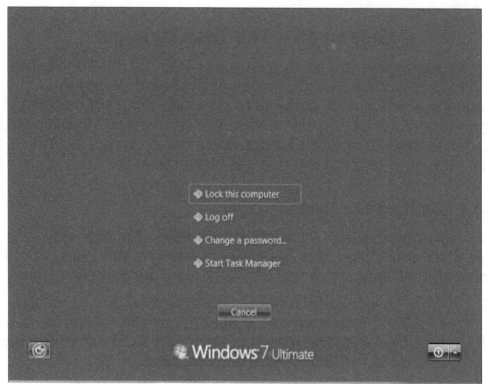

Figure 45.2 – Summon this screen by pressing the Control, Alt and Delete keys together

Choose "Start Task Manager" from the menu to load Task Manger. Figure 45.3 shows Windows Task Manager open on the "Applications" tab:-

Figure 45.3 – Windows Task Manager

45.2 - Managing tasks

The Applications tab shows a list of programs that are currently running. In figure 45.3 we can see Internet Explorer and Windows Media Player. Programs which are running and behaving normally will have a status of "Running". Both Internet Explorer and Windows Media Player are running normally in figure 45.3. Occasionally a program will freeze or stop responding to mouse or keyboard input. When this happens you may need to start the Task Manager to end the program.

A program/task which has stopped responding will be marked

as "Not responding" in the status column. If you cannot end the program normally, select it from the list of tasks in Task Manager and then click the "End Task" button. Windows will then attempt to force the program to exit. You may see a window appear telling you that the application is not responding and that you might lose data if you proceed to force it to close. Any information you were working on in your program that was not saved will probably be lost, but if the application is no longer responding this may be the only course of action you can take.

45.3 - Processes

To access the Processes tab, simply click on it at the top of the Task Manager window. Figure 45.4 shows the Task Manager open on the Processes tab:-

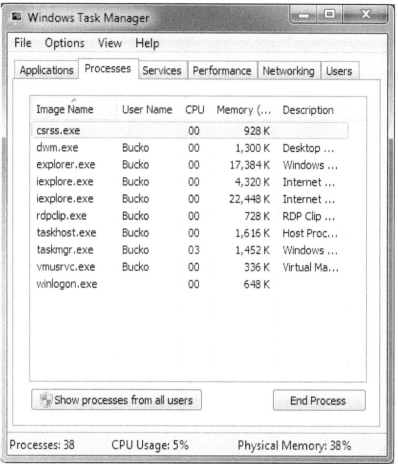

Figure 45.4 – The Processes tab lists all running processes

A process might be an application, either one that is running with a window or hidden in the notification area, or a subsystem or service managed by the operating system.

To see more processes, click on the "Show processes from all users" button. You will need your administrator password if you are running a standard user account.

Just like with tasks, you can end a process by clicking on it from the list and then choosing "End Process". Be careful when ending processes, you will lose any unsaved data in the program. If you end a system process, you might make your computer unstable, forcing you to restart it.

45.4 - Other Task Manager tabs

The other tabs available in the Task Manager can occasionally be useful too, so we will take a quick tour of them now.

The Services tab shows which services are available on your PC. Services add extra functionality to Windows such as networking or CD recording. From this tab you can start and stop services by right clicking on them. We do not recommend doing this unless you are an advanced user and know exactly what you are doing.

The Performance tab shows a graphical representation of computer resource use on your PC. Figure 45.5 shows the Task Manager open on the Performance tab:-

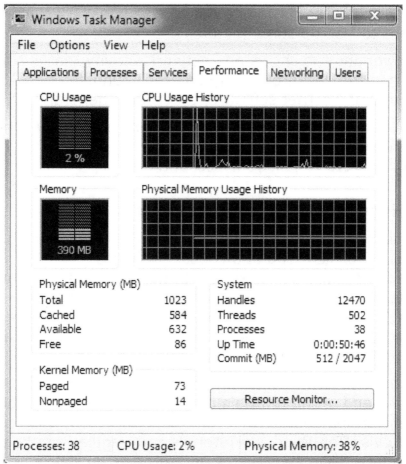

Figure 45.5 – The Performance tab of the Task Manager

You do not need to understand all the technical jargon shown in figure 45.5. The important things to note are CPU Usage and Memory. The CPU usage gauge is an indicator of how much computing work your PC is doing. When your computer is idle on the desktop, you should see around 0% to 3% CPU usage. If there is always some CPU activity going on pushing the meter higher, you may have some spyware or other software running in the background.

The Memory gauge is a measure of how much data the computer is working on at the moment. If this gauge is nearly

337

full, your computer is running out of resources. Try closing some programs to free up some memory.

The Networking tab shows any network activity that is currently going on in the background. If you aren't running any networking or internet software, this should generally be at 0%.

Finally, there is the Users tab. On this tab you can see which users are logged in or connected to your PC. On a home PC this is usually limited to just your account.

45.5 - *Running a program from the Task Manager*

It is possible to run a program from the Task Manager. To do this, open the File menu and choose "New Task (Run...)". You will need to know where the program file is located on your computer however. In some rare instances this can be useful, if you find yourself troubleshooting a serious PC problem the Task Manager may be the only way to run a program if the Start Menu wont open, for example.

This is the last lesson in our PC maintenance section and it marks the end of the tutorials for Windows 7! You have not finished learning about Windows 7 though, no-one ever is. Don't forget to visit Top-Windows-Tutorials.com regularly to keep up with the latest tips, techniques and tutorials for getting the most out of your Windows 7 PC.

In the last chapter we take a brief look at some popular Windows software that is compatible with Windows 7.

Chapter 10 – And Finally...

You now know all about Windows 7, but the real purpose of an operating system is to help you run software. In this last chapter we will discuss some popular software packages that let you accomplish various computing tasks. Remember that there are always plenty of other software recommendations on Top-Windows-Tutorials.com.

Popular Windows Software

You will always be spoilt for choice when looking for software to run on your Windows 7 machine. As the most popular operating system for home computer users, Windows has a software package to suit almost every need. In this final section of the book, we will explore some common home computing tasks and look at some popular software packages that help you with them.

E-mail

Electronic mail (e-mail) has been a popular service since the birth of the internet. Sending messages across the internet electronically is very convenient (if a little insecure). It is possible to access e-mail using just the world wide web and a web browser, but it can be faster and more convenient to do so through a separate e-mail program. The Windows Mail program bundled with Windows Vista has been dropped in Windows 7, but there are several alternatives including:-

Mozilla Thunderbird (Free, see http://www.mozillamessaging.com/en-US/thunderbird/)

Reclaim your inbox with this powerful free e-mail program which includes antispam technologies and is extendible through plug-ins.

Microsoft Outlook ($109.95, see http://office.microsoft.com/en-us/outlook/)

Microsoft's powerful Outlook package includes a professional e-mail package as well as a personal organiser and calendar application. It is the standard PIM (personal information manager) in many businesses.

Games

There are thousands of game titles available for Windows

machines, from easy pick up and play titles to complex and in-depth simulation games.

Image and photograph editing

Working with photographs is something that modern, powerful computers have become very good at. There are several programs that can help you catalogue, edit and enhance your photographs. Below are three of the most popular:-

Adobe Photoshop (from $699,

see http://www.adobe.com/products/photoshop/compare/)

Photoshop remains the image editing program of choice for professional photographers and artists around the world.

Google Picasa (free – see http://picasa.google.com/)

Enhance, catalogue and display your pictures with this popular tool from the search engine giant Google.

Paint (bundled with Windows 7)

Windows 7 includes a basic graphics utility called Paint, which can be used for simple image editing.

Paint.net (free – see http://www.getpaint.net/)

An amazing free graphics package with a feature set that rivals those found in commercially available alternatives.

Windows Live Photo Gallery (free –

see http://download.live.com/photogallery)

Another powerful tool for enhancing and cataloguing your family photos, this time from Microsoft.

Instant messaging, video and voice chat

With an internet connection you can do so much more than just browse the web. Chat to friends and family for free using instant messaging, voice over IP (VOIP) and webcam software (additional hardware may be required for video and voice chat).

Skype (free – see www.skype.com/)

Skype has been the market leader in internet telephony and voice over IP (VOIP) communications for several years now. What that means is, you can use your internet connection to call your friends on Skype for free. You can also use Skype to call normal telephones at rates which are often far cheaper than other services. If you have a webcam, you can also video chat with your Skype friends too!

Trillian (basic version is free – see http://www.trillian.im/)

There are several popular instant messaging services in use on the internet today. If you have friends on several services, Trillian can connect to them all through one handy interface.

Windows Live Messenger (free – see http://download.live.com/messenger)

A very popular messaging utility which also supports voice and video chat with compatible hardware. Windows Live Messenger is also compatible with Live Family Safety, enabling parents to regulate their children's online activities and contacts.

Music and Multimedia

Windows Media Player and Media Center are not the only ways your Windows 7 PC can sing and dance. There is plenty of great software out there that can help you discover your media in new and exciting ways.

Boxee (free – see http://www.boxee.tv/)

Discover a huge range of internet TV shows, including broadcasts of popular shows and special interest programming.

As well as being the best internet TV browser, Boxee can catalogue your media files too. A great alternative to Windows Media Center.

Winamp (basic version is free – see http://www.winamp.com/)

Winamp remains one of the most popular alternatives to Windows Media Player. With a streamlined interface and support for a huge range of plug-ins as well as integrated internet radio stations.

VLC (free – see www.videolan.org/vlc/)

VLC is a popular media player with a low memory and processor overhead that is renowned for its high compatibility with a wide range of media files.

Music creation

Want to make sweet music with your PC? There are plenty of software packages that can help with that too.

Cakewalk SONAR Home Studio (from $139.99 – see http://www.cakewalk.com/products/homestudio/)

SONAR Home Studio 7 is the easiest way to turn your PC into a full-fledged music production studio. From start to finish, SONAR Home Studio will help you capture your creativity and share it with the world. With SONAR Home Studio you can record live instruments, vocals, or any audio source (compatible hardware permitting).

Sound Forge (from $54.95 – see http://www.sonycreativesoftware.com/soundforgesoftware)

Sound Forge Audio Studio software is the easiest way to record, edit, encode, and master audio on your PC. Includes vinyl recording and restoration to help you convert those precious old records (compatible hardware permitting).

Online safety

Children love to explore the internet, but not everything and everyone they encounter is suitable for them. Windows 7 includes a family safety module, but it needs to work in conjunction with other software to be really effective.

Windows Live Family Safety (free – see http://download.live.com/familysafety)

This family safety package integrates with Windows Explorer and Windows Live Messenger to help protect children from strangers and unsuitable content on the web.

Optenet (From $39.95 – See http://www.optenetpc.com/)

Optenet PC is a highly effective internet filter which can filter adult and unsuitable content with minimal false positives and without making your internet run slowly.

Web browsing

Internet Explorer is not the only way to get around the web!

Mozilla Firefox (free – see http://www.mozilla.com/firefox/)

Firefox is the most popular alternative to Internet Explorer. Faster, safer, and smarter, Firefox also has a huge range of plug-ins that can be used to extend and customise the browser.

Google Chrome (free – see http://www.google.com/chrome)

Google Chrome is rapidly catching up with Firefox in the popularity stakes, it's known for its super fast browsing speeds and simple, uncluttered interface.

Word processing and office

Microsoft Office (from $149 – see http://office.microsoft.com/)

The de-facto standard Office suite for many businesses, colleges and universities. Includes the industry standard word processor, Microsoft Word and probably the most powerful spreadsheet package in the world, Microsoft Excel.

OpenOffice.org (free – see http://www.openoffice.org/)

A fantastic Microsoft office compatible productivity suite that is completely free! What's more, you can purchase our OpenOffice.org Writer Superguide and learn how to produce professional looking documents with Writer. This book was written using OpenOffice.org Writer! To learn more, see http://www.top-windows-tutorials.com/openoffice-writer.html.

www.ingramcontent.com/pod-product-compliance
Lightning Source LLC
Chambersburg PA
CBHW080152060326
40689CB00018B/3951